THE BIG BOOK OF

TopGear

2011

BOOKS

James May's Splendid things Calendar

MAY

SUNDAY   MONDAY   TU

Mother

IMPROVEMENT SYSTEM

Koala Bears

Problem: **Lazy**
Solution: **Jet-Pack Arms**

Pandas

Problem: **Hard to move**
Solution: **Wheels**

Cats

Problem: **Idle**
Solution: **Robot Legs**

Sloths

Forget it

THE HAMMOND NATURE

Tortoises
Problem: **Slow**
Solution: **Jet Engines**

Swans
Problem: **Listless**
Solution: **Outboard Motors**

Red Kites
Problem: **Aimless circles**
Solution: **Propellors**

Donkeys
Problem: **Plodding**
Solution: **Superchargers**

Yard Full of Rusty Cars House
The Countryside
Hairgel, HL9 5SK

Dr Hugh Beard
Animal Management Director
London Zoo
London

13 September 2010

Dear Sir,

I recently took my children on an outing to your zoo, and I have
to say that whilst some aspects of the trip were indeed
enlightening - who knew giraffes had such long necks! - I found
the experience as a whole rather underwhelming. Having given
the matter some thought on the way home, I think I have put my
finger on the problem. Basically, all the animals aren't as good
as they could be. Nature has come up short and left mankind
staring at a bunch of creatures that still need a bit of work.
Please find enclosed my proposal for The Hammond Nature
Improvement System, which as you'll see from only a quick
perusal, is eminently workable. If only Isaac Newton had
thought of this. Or was it Darwin?

I look forward to hearing from you, and here's to no more Bank
Holidays with glum kids' faces!

Yours sincerely,

Richard Hammond.

POTENTIAAAAAA

HOUSE OF
CLARKSON

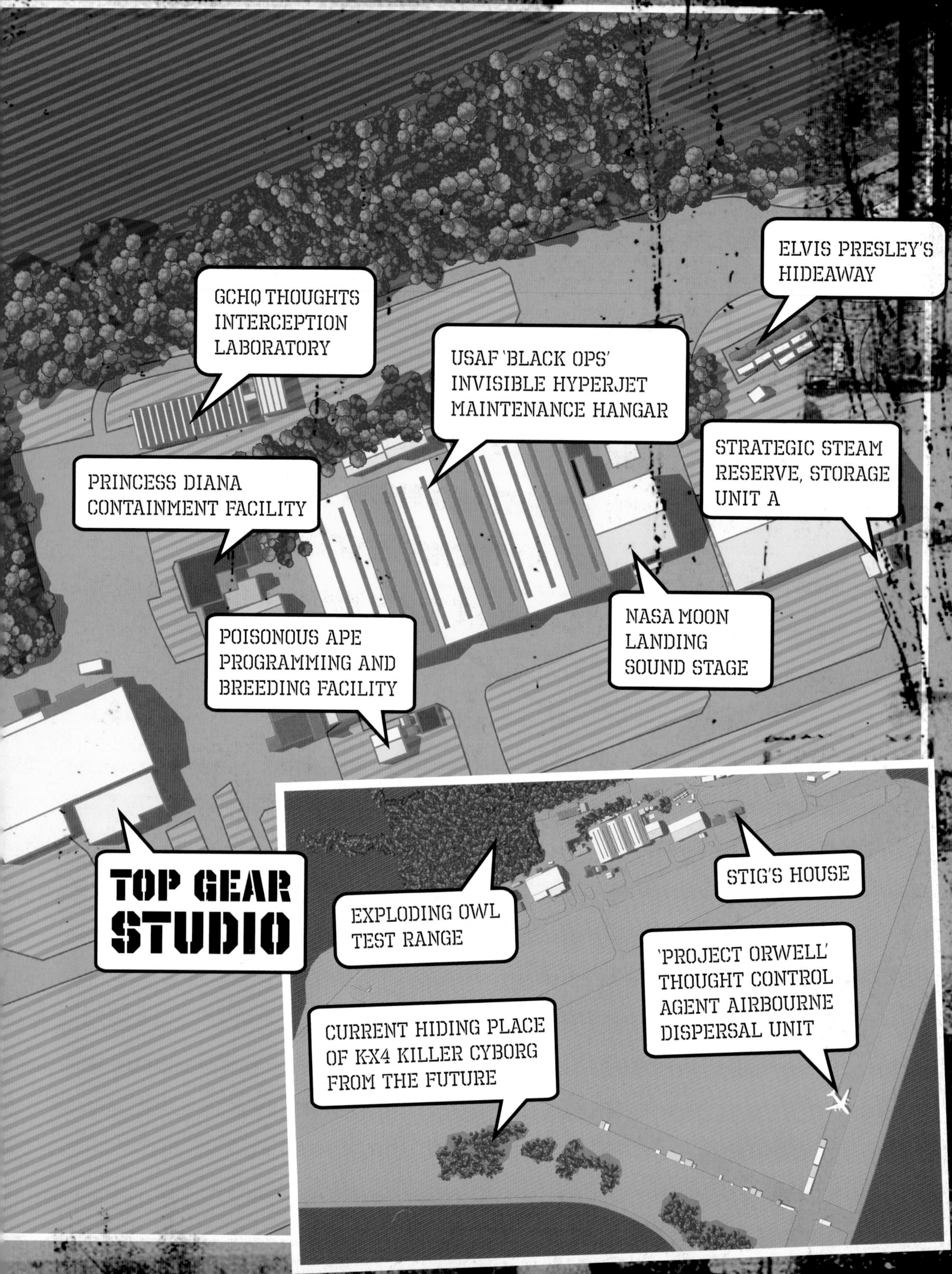
GCHQ THOUGHTS INTERCEPTION LABORATORY
USAF 'BLACK OPS' INVISIBLE HYPERJET MAINTENANCE HANGAR
ELVIS PRESLEY'S HIDEAWAY
STRATEGIC STEAM RESERVE, STORAGE UNIT A
PRINCESS DIANA CONTAINMENT FACILITY
NASA MOON LANDING SOUND STAGE
POISONOUS APE PROGRAMMING AND BREEDING FACILITY
TOP GEAR STUDIO
STIG'S HOUSE
EXPLODING OWL TEST RANGE
'PROJECT ORWELL' THOUGHT CONTROL AGENT AIRBOURNE DISPERSAL UNIT
CURRENT HIDING PLACE OF K-X4 KILLER CYBORG FROM THE FUTURE

SECRETS OF DUNSFOLD

THE AIRFIELD WHERE TOP GEAR IS FILMED APPEARS TO BE COVERED IN NOTHING MORE THAN BORING WAREHOUSES AND LIGHT-ENGINEERING WORKSHOPS. BUT THAT'S EXACTLY WHAT THEY WANT YOU TO THINK...

SAS EXTREME COMBAT UNIT

MI5 VAMPIRE PRISON UNIT

CIA'S UK & EUROPE ALIEN AUTOPSY CENTER

SAS EXTREME CATERING UNIT

Supercars

The fastest, the silliest and, frankly, the most brilliant cars of all

FERRARI F40

Despite being made in part from fancy materials like Kevlar and carbon fibre, the F40 was not a sophisticated car. It had no traction control, no computerized suspension, no power steering. Instead of interior door handles it had bits of string, like an old Mini, and never mind anti-lock brakes – it didn't even have a brake servo. It was just a brutal 2.9-litre, 478bhp, twin-turbo V8 in a lightweight body. And that's why it was also the most pure and exhilarating petrolhead experience short of injecting super unleaded straight into an artery.

BUGATTI VEYRON

If you watch *Top Gear* you probably know all about the Veyron. How it has 10 radiators, one of them just to cool the rear wing's hydraulics. How that wing itself is capable of flipping up to generate the same deceleration as the actual brakes on a Fiesta. How every part of the car is so lavishly made that even the indicator stalk costs over £2000. The fact the Veyron even exists is an amazing thing and, to paraphrase John F Kennedy's famous words about the race to the moon, it's all down to the engineers who choose to do it, not because it was easy, but because it was hard.

MCLAREN F1

Like the Veyron, there's almost nothing that hasn't been said about the F1. Nonetheless, you couldn't leave it out of a list like this, even if Jeremy doesn't like it very much. But instead of repeating all that stuff about 'gold-lined engine bay... central driving position... blah blah blah...' we'll give you one example of the relentless perfectionism that went into the F1: to this day, more than 18 years after it was revealed, designer Gordon Murray still loses sleep over the positioning of the switch that activates the engine compartment light. Now *that's* attention to detail.

PAGANI ZONDA

Supercar world can be a pretty snobbish place. The Honda NSX, for example, is rarely considered a 'proper supercar' because it doesn't have enough cylinders or a pedigree badge on the front. Lamborghini isn't seen as entirely in the same league as Ferrari because it lacks the necessary motor racing heritage. So when a bloke called Mr Pagani announced a supercar with a tuned-up Mercedes engine and no racing background whatsoever you could forgive the snobs for sniggering. Then they saw it. And heard it. And drove it. And the sniggering stopped forever.

PORSCHE 959

The 959 arrived around the same time as the Ferrari F40, yet to compare the two cars was like taking a cheese to a chalk festival. Where the Italians made a machine of remarkable simplicity, the Germans had whipped up a techno festival of the like not seen since they invented Kraftwerk. It had four-wheel drive, electronically controlled shock absorbers, a tyre-pressure monitoring system, and headlight washers that retracted so they didn't spoil the aerodynamics. In fact, it had all the things you'd expect to find on a supercar designed in 2011. But it had them in 1986. Amazing.

LAMBOURGHINI COUNTACH

There are a few things you want from a true supercar. A shape that's modelled on an especially exciting wedge of cheese. An engine with 12 cylinders that makes a noise like a scalded dinosaur. An almost deliberate absence of practicality, rear visibility and anything that might be mistaken for sensibleness. Rarity is good too, because a supercar should be an unusual thrill to spot in the street, not something you run into every other day. Oh, and slightly mad doors. A supercar really ought to have slightly mad doors. Put all those together and you've got the Countach. The textbook.

Richard Hammond's
Guide to the Countryside

The British countryside can be a strange and confusing place, especially if you're a born and bred townie. Thankfully, Top Gear's own Richard Hammond lives deep in the heart of somewhere-near-Wales and with his help we are uniquely placed to guide you through some of the charming customs and distinctive rules of those places where it's basically impossible to find a cash machine or somewhere that sells coffee.

What does the countryside look like?

◀ No. This is a park. It's what townies might think is the countryside but it isn't. Awful.

▶ That's better. This is the real countryside. Lovely.

Driving in the countryside

Thems city folks would make the mistake of driving fancy 4x4s like Range Rovers and thinking they's going to blend into the countryside. If you wants to do that, first you have to fit the following to your car:
- Rust
- Smell of dog
- Red diesel

What to wear in the countryside

City folks always make the mistake of wearing a wax jacket and Wellingtons and fancy townie things like glasses. If you want to blend in out in the countryside, you should have:
- Overalls
- Dad's boots
- One eye

Names that them city folk might use

- John • Sarah • Chris

Names that be of the country an' that

- Bungo • Jed Mental • One-Eye Dave

Animals you might see in the countryside

Lunch   Lunch   Snack   Lunch

Making friends in the countryside

You should respect the rules of the countryside, even if you do not understand them and suspect that people in the countryside keep changing those rules just to annoy you. In your attempts to make friends, please remember that the following will not work in the countryside:
- Ostentatious shows of spelling ability
- Attempts to show off recent dental work
- Your mobile phone

FOREWORD
BY
THE STIG

THE BIG BOOK OF TOP GEAR
CONTENTS

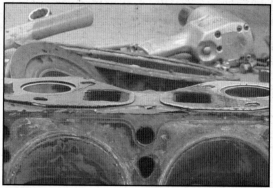

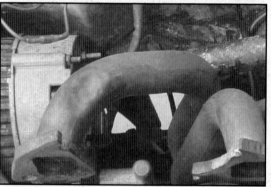

'LITERALLY AWFUL'
The Sun

'NOISY AND POINTLESS'
The Daily Mirror

'SODDING BRILLIANT!'
The London Review of Books

LEONARDO DICAPRIO
as Richard Hammond

MATT DAMON
as Jeremy Clarkson

DAME JUDI DENCH
as James May

TOP GEAR THE MOVIE

Three people. Three cars. One pointless journey.

In a post-apocalyptic world, only three guys could discover if it was possible to buy practical but powerful hatchback cars for less than the cost of a new compact and then drive them across Englandland for no real reason, undertaking a series of challenges along the way.

20th Century Stig presents
TOP GEAR — THE MOVIE
Matt Damon   Leonardo DiCaprio   Dame Judi Dench as James May   Featuring Ross Kemp as The Man In The Trunk
Produced by Don Weaselburger & Jack Tungsten   Written by Alan Smithee   Directed by Chip Cutfast
Vehicles provided by eBay   Costumes courtesy of Oxfam   Catering by Ginsters of Cornwall
Mr DiCaprio's hair by Through A Hedge Backwards of Ledbury   Mr Damon's hair by Perm-u-Like Ltd.

Filmed in Hollywood, CA and on location just outside Birmingham, UK

 DOLBY SYSTEM
DOLBY HX PRO

 Distributed by HHCIB Pictures and Oh Cock! inc.

 15

AN APOLOGY
by James May

Hello. I was asked to write the introduction to this latest
Big Book of Top Gear, which normally I would be happy to do. Instead,
however, I find myself forced to make an apology.

I don't deny that this book is loosely concerned with the popular BBC2
car-based sit-com *Top Gear*, but it isn't really especially big, is it? It's
almost exactly the same size as *The Beano Book*, which has been around
for decades and has never been called *The Big Book of The Beano*.

Yes, *The Big Book of Top Gear* is bigger than a typical novel when viewed
from the front, but it's also thinner. Equally, it's nowhere near as thick as the
average Bible and you never see those advertised as *The Big Book of the Bible*.

The fact is that when compared with other faintly comedic and picture-
led annuals, *The Big Book of Top Gear* has to be considered only
averagely dimensioned. It should therefore really be called *The Normal
Sized (by the standards of other comparable volumes on sale during
the festive period) Book of Top Gear.*

Unfortunately I have been told that this would not look as good on the
cover which is why, for the third year running, this average-sized book
labours under a frankly misleading title.

For this, and everything else you're about to read, I apologize.

James May

PEOPLE JEREMY HAS OFFENDED

- Germans
- Poles
- Muslims
- Greeks
- Romanians
- Australians
- Malaysians
- South Koreans
- Motorcyclists
- Lorry drivers
- Peugeot drivers
- Gay people
- Old people
- The Welsh
- The Scottish
- The lesbian
- South African wine makers
- Gordon Brown
- Rover enthusiasts
- Speed camera fans
- Eco-mentalists
- The Welsh (again)

THE WORLD

The 2010 World Cup wasn't especially interesting for anyone, least of all England fans. So *Top Gear* decided to put together a rather different tournament that would help rekindle some national pride...

Sweden V Russia

A fixture steeped in historical meaning, according to Wikipedia, and it's an easy victory for the energetic – if entirely deranged – Swede, crushing the lumbering Soviet with a devastating blend of raw power, raw pace and raw herring.

LADA RIVA

VOLVO C30 POLESTAR

Germany V Spain

SEAT EXEO

A mouth-watering match up between the dependable Teutonic workhorse and, er, a very slightly older version of the same dependable Teutonic workhorse. Spain turns out to be far better at football than cars.

AUDI A4

Germany V Sweden

KOENIGSEGG CCX

Showing a lack of balance on the wing, the bonkers Swede crashes out against the brilliant German with its dash of suspiciously Italian flair. Never write off the Germans.

AUDI R8 V10

HSV COMMODORE

USA V Australia

A brawny, unsophisticated grudge match between the former colonies ends with a bruising victory for the hairy-chested Camaro. And 14 broken legs, a missing eye and a large unexplained fire.

CHEVROLET CAMARO

England V Germany

PORSCHE 911 GT3 RS

The grudge match. The big one. The predictable references to wars and sun loungers. And it inevitably ends in an agonising penalty defeat for the Brit, the penalty in question being a three-point fine for entering a bus lane before 7pm.

CHRYSLER 300C

England V USA

An easy victory for the big, classy Brit over the shady Yank. Some say it's unfair to match a £70k superlimo against a £30k Mafia saloon, but hey, we don't make the rules...

A HORSE

Germany VE[...]

The one they all wanted to see: the two top supercars of the year, conveniently brought together through the miracle of gentle match-fixing. Despite

MERCEDES SLS

England V North Korea

Despite giving away a little in top speed to the shadowy Communist, the plucky Brit wins through with a dependable performance in muddy conditions. And resilience to the Venezuelan equine encephalitis virus unfortunately found in the half-time oranges.

JAGUAR XJ

ASTON V12 VANTAGE

LAND ROVER DEFENDER

CUP OF CARS

...Our initial proposal, involving a hungry bull mastiff, five gallons of Bisto and an arquebus was rejected, so we came up with this instead. Yes, sorry, we still end up losing to the Germans.

ALFA BRERA

Italy V South Korea

KIA CEE'D

The Reasonably Priced Korean – despite recent experience on the international stage – can't keep pace with the silky Italian with the lovely bottom. Our metaphor is beginning to struggle, isn't it? Sorry.

RENAULTSPORT CLIO

France V China

The tiny tenacious terrier from, er, Viry-Chatillon dishes out a lesson in manners to the oriental oddity, but expect a stronger showing from the Chinese next time round.

TANG HUA DETROIT FISH

FIAT 500

Italy V France

A close-fought battle between these two chi-chi Europeans, and it's the retro Italian that heads through to the next round because, er, we've run out of interesting French cars. Sorry.

CITROEN DS3

NISSAN GTR

Japan V Holland

Sophisticated technical precision versus interesting design, and it's the GTR that wins through, inflicting a nasty neck injury on its opponent in the process.

SPYKER AILERON

GAZAL 1

LAMBORGHINI MURCIELAGO SV

Italy V Japan

It's the battle of the big hitters, but the LFA's technical precision is no match for the mad passion of the Murcielago, which takes the win by SHOUTING REALLY LOUDLY and being quite scary.

HONDA S2000

Japan V Romania

Bad news! The tenacious little Sandero is dumped out in the quarter-finals by the ageing S2000, in its final tournament before retiring. Back to the international wilderness for the Dacia.

LEXUS LFA

SUS **Italy**

...the SLS using its (gull) wings to good advantage, it's the silky all-round skills of the 458 that win out, clinching the inaugural Car World Cup for the Italians. Vittoria!

FERRARI 458

DACIA SANDERO

Suadi Arabia V Romania

Good news! The spunky Sandero comes through unscathed against the minty Middle Eastern upstart. World domination beckons. Affordable, understated world domination.

DACIA SANDERO

TOO TERRIBLE FOR TV

Every long-running TV show has its duff ideas, its clunky thoughts, its silly notions that shouldn't get any further than a scrawl on a note pad. In this respect *Top Gear* is no different. It's just that sometimes *Top Gear* accidentally goes ahead and films these bad ideas, edits them into a neat package and then belatedly realizes that they're rubbish and should not be shown on television. For the first time anywhere, we can now open the vault door on some of these useless and never-to-be-seen *Top Gear* white elephants.

Fiat Panda Armoured Car

On paper this was a great challenge: can you make a cut-price armoured car out of an old Fiat Panda? Hammond set off to find out. Unfortunately, whilst his armoured car itself was full of inspired thinking, the various attempts to test the toughness of his creation were beset by problems, mostly involving things that were meant to look spectacular but actually looked a bit lame. Add in a late re-edit that changed the order of the tests, thereby introducing a clanging continuity error that made a shattered window magically mend itself then break again, and you've got an item that promised much but never quite worked out. The actual Panda, by the way, languished in the TG boneyard for years afterwards until someone had the presence of mind to get rid of it.

Lotus Europa

A new Lotus is always a cause for excitement. Except the Europa wasn't really a new Lotus, it was just the old Elise chassis lightly re-clothed and fitted with an interior that was meant to be luxurious but was actually as lavish as a party in a prison. Jeremy did his best to make a good track test out of it but, frankly, with a car as irrelevant (and ultimately unsuccessful) as this, he was fighting a losing battle and the TG office decided not to waste anyone's time by showing it on television.

The Top Gear Bus

Inspired by those beer adverts, someone came up with the idea that *Top Gear* doesn't do public transport... but if they did it would be the best in the world. Armed with this simple premise, a cheap Routemaster bus was bought before Richard and James were dispatched to help equip it with various gag devices and set-ups that would make each journey on it more pleasurable. Thing is, they were rubbish. So rubbish that Hammond and May could barely keep a straight face during filming and the finished item was so comically cack that they begged the producer to bin it for everyone's sake. The poor old Routemaster languished in the TG car park for years afterwards, known to everyone on the team by the name Richard and James had coined for it. It was called simply 'The Unfunny Bus'.

BMW 6-series Convertible

Back in 2004 it was decided that Hammond really ought to get out on the track and make a power test for the next series. Unfortunately, it seemed Jeremy had already tested all the powerful, exciting cars and the only thing Richard could find to film was the then-new BMW 6-series cabriolet. So, a not very interesting variant on a car *Top Gear* was never very interested in. As you can guess, the end result didn't make for very interesting viewing. That's why it's never been shown.

Pontiac Solstice

Jeremy was going to the United States to race his PlayStation self around a real track in Northern California. While he's there, the TG team thought, we might as well get him to bang in a road test for the next series as well. Unfortunately, the only car they could think of for Clarkson to test was this dismal roadster that wasn't even likely to be sold in Britain and was therefore largely irrelevant. Hence enthusiasm was pretty low and it got even lower when Jeremy actually drove it and realized it was awful. The test was filmed but since there didn't seem to be much point to it, it was stuck on the shelf for ages and then eventually consigned to the bin.

...ension or expansion? **p21**

PROVIDES WARMTH TO THE INTERIOR OF A BUILDING

central heating

FURNACE of the week!

TYPICAL EFFICIENCIES FOR CENTRAL HEATING ARE 85-97%!

Spotted!
James May arriving at the MOBO Awards in a fake fur coat and a massive gold necklace with an 18-PERSON ENTOURAGE behind him!

Spotted!
James May and Dappy FROM N-DUBZ hanging out together at Spektekal club in London!

Overheard!
James May telling UNA FROM THE SATURDAYS that DJ Armin Van Buuren's recent Creamfields gig 'was some real phat shit man!'

Spotted!
James May and Paris Hilton GETTING ON A YACHT in Sardinia with six bikini-clad girls and a man carrying an enormous box of Cristal Champagne!

Overheard!
James May in a posh, central-London restaurant telling HIS DINING COMPANION, singer Avril Lavigne, that 'me and Pharrell are working on some cool shit together'.

Spotted!
James May and Abby Clancy going for a day spa at an exclusive hotel IN CHESHIRE!

Spotted!
James May dancing on the terrace at Hyporia club in Ibiza UNTIL 5AM!

Spotted!
James May GOING INTO a hardware shop in Hammersmith to buy some wood screws.

The Hammerhead
Eagle i-Thrust

Owners ~~Manuel~~
Manual

Introduction

Thank you for purchasing this Hammerhead Eagle i-Thrust electrically powered car.
You have chosen wisely, and we are confident that this vehicle will give you many
hours, days and perhaps even weeks of service as a cheaper and significantly less
embarrassing alternative to a G-Wiz or one of those other awful electric cars with
a pathetically fake eco name like 'mosstech' or 'e-chrysanthemum' or something.
Please read this manual carefully. It may help to prevent you getting electrocuted
or careering down a small hill and into a tree.

GETTING INTO THE CAR
The Hammereagle Thrust i-Head is just like a normal car, despite being electrically
powered. The doors are perfectly normal, it's just that they don't fit very well and
we may have forgotten to include any way of locking them. Also, some of the edges are
quite sharp and may cause your fingers to 'fall off'. So do watch out for that.

THE CONTROLS
The dashboard of the Hammerthrust Head-i Eagle demonstrates the benefits of
simplification that electric power can bring. As we know, an electric motor
contains very few moving parts. Likewise, the dashboard of this car contains very
little equipment. The diagram below shows the basics.

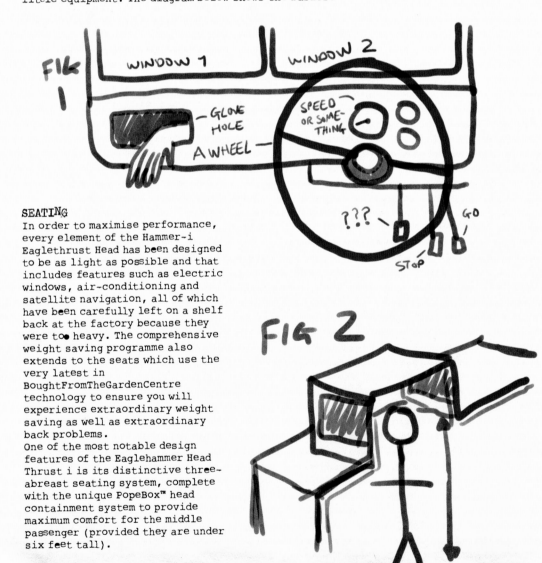

SEATING
In order to maximise performance,
every element of the Hammer-i
Eaglethrust Head has been designed
to be as light as possible and that
includes features such as electric
windows, air-conditioning and
satellite navigation, all of which
have been carefully left on a shelf
back at the factory because they
were too heavy. The comprehensive
weight saving programme also
extends to the seats which use the
very latest in
BoughtFromTheGardenCentre
technology to ensure you will
experience extraordinary weight
saving as well as extraordinary
back problems.
One of the most notable design
features of the Eaglehammer Head
Thrust i is its distinctive three-
abreast seating system, complete
with the unique PopeBox™ head
containment system to provide
maximum comfort for the middle
passenger (provided they are under
six feet tall).

How the PopeBox™ system works: you get in, then put your head in it. The PopeBox™ is the result of many hours of careful computer-aided design and is in no way just a transparent plastic storage box turned upsidedown and crudely gaffer taped over a hole cut in the roof.

STARTING THE ENGINE
The Headeagle Thrust-i-Hammer starts on a key, just like any other car. However, when the key is first turned you will hear no engine noise. Do not be alarmed. Unless it turns out that the engine has also caught fire. Then you should be slightly alarmed.

SETTING OFF
To set off simply engage going forward mode. Ignore the clutch, we just forgot to take that off when we bought that Fiat Panda pedal box from the scrapyard. Depressing the accelerator will commence forward motion. Depressing your fellow presenters will commence as soon as they realise this car isn't very fast.

PERFORMANCE
The i-Headhammer Thrust Eagle has been independently performance-tested by Autocar magazine. Unfortunately we seem to have lost that particular copy of Autocar and can't remember what their figures are so we've asked Jeremy to come up with some estimates.

0-30mph - 0.5sec / 0-60mph - 1.5sec / Top speed - 280mph

HANDLING
The Hammer-iHead Eager Thrush features a rear-biased weight balance, just like other highly respected performance cars such as the Porsche 911, the Porsche 911, or another sort of Porsche 911. This results in excellent balance, agility, maneuverability and an almost complete absence of undesirable traits like suddenly flying off the road for no apparent reason whilst trying to drive in a straight line.
Oh yeah, Jeremy's just remembered the Renault Alpine. That had its engine at the back too and it was a massive success as a result.
Unlike so many of today's sanitised and over-complicated so-called "driver's cars" the Thurstammer Iagle Heads-E does not use power steering. This allows the driver to feel connected to the road. Unless he touches the metal steering column, in which case what he will feel connected to is the batteries.

THE HYBRID DRIVE SOLUTION SYSTEM
The Thirst-I Eagle Homohead boasts a unique hybrid drive system which allows it to 'top up' its batteries whilst on the move. The system uses a whisper-quiet diesel generator sourced from well-respected powertrain provider Pete From The Travelling Fair Ltd. If, whilst driving along, the driver detects a loss of power or sudden slowing of his Belinda Carlisle cassette, he can simply pull over and activate the on-board generator, having first put on the breathing apparatus provided.

SAFETY
The MC Hammer EgoThrushHead-i has been designed with your safety in mind and tested to the extremes at the top secret MIRA proving ground somewhere in Leicestershire, just off the A5 near Caldecote and Fenny Drayton. Peace of mind in the unlikely event that you find yourself driving very very slowly towards a concrete wall and then subsequently discover that footage of this event has been speeded up using the Avid computerised editing system.

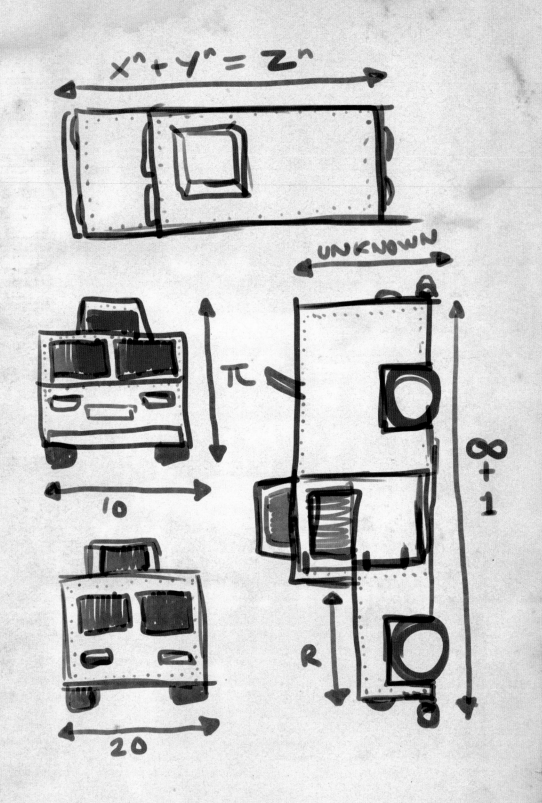

He's back!

All the latest bangin' choons straight outta Hammersmith!

MC J May is mixin' up a phat one!

What Gramaphone? magazine

WELL THIS IS SMASHING

SLAMMIN'!

Simon Rattle

The ornamentations of his Baroque-style basslines are SICK!

Michael Nyman

—ANTHEMS VOL. 1—

RAVEY MAY

Featuring...

Entropy (Squeeze Me Hat Mix) by Juice Hooty!

Symphony No. 4 in E minor by Brahms!

Xelon 7 (Garage Massive In Space Edit) by Brother Robot Cat!

Concerto for Piano and Orchestra No. 1 in F sharp minor by Rachmaninov!

Laser Face Jelly Taste (Crispy Biscuits Mix) by Joost Poo!

Piano Sonata No. 15 in D by Beethoven!

Melting Love Trouser (Opal Fruits Remix) by Chegwin!

Linear Line Test Noise Whisper (Alesto Mix) by Allegro Van Den Plas!

Pomp and Circumstance, Op.39: March, No.4 in G by Elgar!

ChimmyChonger On The Bonger (Lucy's Weasel Edit) by BUNG!

Capriccio Espagnol, Op.34 'Scena e canto gitano' by Rimsky-Korsakov!

CLARKSON HYPERBOLE SERVICE

FROM THE DESK OF:
JULES VERNE
DUNDIVIN' 322 RUE DE PAMPLEMOUSSE, PARIS 76433

2 February 1896

Jeremy,

I have almost completed work on the novel I consider to be my masterpiece. However, I have the concern that the title is not exciting enough. Can you help?

The book, she is called "One or Maybe Two Leagues Under The Sea"

Yours Sincerely,
Jules

Take That
The Take That Treehouse
Manchestur
M1 6GD
3 November 1991

Dear Jeremy

I have written this new song for my pop group TAKE THAT which I think is really good but I am a bit worried that it's lacking a certain something

The song is called "Three love songs"
Hope you can help,

GARY BARLOW

One or maybe two? No, no, no.
TWENTY THOUSAND Leagues.
Jeremy

HIGH STREET, SHOUTING, OXON

Saab Sverige
Sensibergenplazz 17, Krumple
166 22 Airbaggen
Sweden

17 July 1985

Dear Jeremy

We have an exciting new car coming out soon and we thought we would go back to our roots by calling it the 91. Can you think of anything to add to that?

All the best,
SAAB

Oh for God's sake, three?
It should be A MILLION love songs.
Jeremy

42,000,0... ...ING, OXON

Oh my God, you idiots. 91???
Wrong, wrong, wrong.
Call it the SAAB 9000
J

42,000,000 MASSIVELY HIGH STREET, SHOUTING, OXON

steven spielberg
2454 Duel Street, Hollywood, CA

Hi Jeremy,

Great news! Harrison Ford has signed
up do a sequel to Raiders Of The
Lost Ark! Think we're gonna call it
'Indiana Jones & The Fairly Scary
Church'. What do you reckon?

Steven

Jerry Bruckheimer
3933 Exploding Boulevard,
Slo-Mo, CA

Hey JC,

Thanks again for your help with Tom
Cruise jet pilot project. You were right,
'Guys Who Are Real Good At Flying
Airplanes' was a lousy title. Glad we
went with your suggestion.

Good news is, Cruise is on board for
a new movie about race car drivers.
Thinking of calling it 'A Few Minutes
Of Light Drizzle'. Whaddya think?

JB

POST CARD
1043 Wookie Road, Modesto, CA, THX1138

CORRESPONDENCE HERE

Jeremy,

I've had a totally awesome idea
for a movie set in a universe
quite far away and I'm thinking
of calling it 'SPACE FIGHT'.
Any suggestions?

George

NAME AND ADDRESS HERE

To Clarkson's Hyperbole Service
42,000,000
Massively High street,
shouting,
Oxon

CLARKSON HYPERBOLE SERVICE

Right, you've got a
<u>MAJOR</u> problem here
Broccoli. This whole Bond franchise
is going to hell in a handcart and
I'll show you why...

Jewels are fairly long lived? No,
no, no. DIAMONDS ARE FOREVER

Live and let live? WRONG Live and let <u>DIE</u>

You could sort of wound him from here?
Give me strength. A VIEW to a KILL.

Certificate to hurt people?? what is
wrong with you? Licence to KILL.

Come back when I'm better? I'm losing
patience with you now. It's DIE Another Day

Quantum of Solace? I'm sorry,
that's Just BOLLOCKS

42,000,000 MASSIVELY HIGH STREET, SHOUTING, OXON

We like the Chevrolet Camaro on Top Gear. Well, Hammond does. But even he would admit that it's not the most sophisticated thing in the world, and nor are the people who drive it. Hence we present...

THINGS YOU'RE UNLIKELY TO HEAR SOMEONE SAYING AS THEY GET INTO THEIR CHEVROLET CAMARO

D'IFFERENTIAL

une fragrance par Richard Hammond

Pour l'homme avec L'and Rover

D'ifferential
une fragrance par Richard Hammond

D'IFFERENTIAL. Une parfum pour l'homme et aussi un bon fluide de power steering. Ne permettez pas le contact avec les yeux. Ne permettez pas le contact avec skin. Si swallowé, cherchez l'aide médicale immediatellement. Si utilize pour le removale du stains, premier test sur un patch conceale. L'utilisation prolonged causé le thinning du cheveux et aussi blindness. © 2010. D'IFFERENTIAL est un registered trademark de Richard Hammond du Ledbury.

 The Inaccurate Movie Database

Search [   ] Go

Movies ▾   TV ▾   News ▾   Video ▾   Community ▾

Blade Runner v2.0 (2008)

Director: Richard Hammond

Plot: Retired LAPD police officer Rick Deckard is called back to duty to deal with a major problem, this time in Gloucestershire. An underlying panic has developed with news that there are people in the village who are not as they first appear. These people are not from round these parts and may be 'townies'. Deckard must identify them and then look at them in a funny way all evening until they feel uncomfortable and leave the pub.

Genre: Inbred   **User Rating:** ★⯪☆☆☆☆☆☆☆

Edward Scissorhands 2 (2007)

Director: Richard Hammond

Plot: The once lonely and outcast Edward begins to feel more at home in the world, especially after he discovers a unique use for his strange hands – opening supermarkets! With a lucrative career of snipping the ribbon, not just shops but also on school extensions, new leisure centres and revamped car showrooms, Edward finds the work is rolling in and eventually lands himself a daytime chat show on ITV. At least until an embarrassing incident with Dame Judi Dench…

Genre: Shameless   **User Rating:** ★★⯪☆☆☆☆☆☆

The Matrix Relocated (2009)

Director: Richard Hammond

Plot: Neo has managed to unplug himself from the Matrix and awakes in unfamiliar surroundings, his eyes alighting on the incredibly floral curtains, the excessively patterned carpet, the knick-knacks left all over the mantelshelf. Slowly he realises he is in a B&B near Ross-on-Wye. His worst fears have come true and now he must escape from the countryside. But he can't because he's dressed like a townie and no one will give him useful directions.

Genre: Unfriendly   **User Rating:** ★⯪☆☆☆☆☆☆☆

Batman Gives In (2006)

Director: Richard Hammond

Plot: Tired of the corruption in Gotham City, Bruce Wayne moves to a small village near Gloucester seeking a quiet life. Sadly, his hopes are dashed when somebody tears all the paper off the noticeboard outside the church hall. To find the culprit Wayne dons his famous bat suit but the locals don't want the help of his fancy city ways. Also, he immediately becomes the subject of an investigation by the Bat Protection League which turns out to involve a lot of paperwork.

Genre: Meddling   **User Rating:** ★⯪☆☆☆☆☆☆☆

Carry On Camping Again (2010)

Director: Richard Hammond

Plot: Kenneth Shaftcock and his lovely wife Jeanette buy an innovative new Land Rover-based camper van that folds out into a house and set off for a weekend in the country where there are no hilarious mishaps or delightful misunderstandings because the whole thing works surprisingly well, unlike the people in the surrounding pitches, Dick Strap with his idiotic Citroen tower block, and Paul Balls with some sort of stupid Lotus. Just to re-iterate, the Land Rover campervan was fine. It was FINE. The end.

Genre: Draughty   **User Rating:** ★★⯪☆☆☆☆☆☆

FLIGHT OF THE CARAVAN AIRSHIP...

"This is Golf Tango Oscar Papa Golf, heading in a westerly direction... no, easterly... erm... the one to the right..."

"Golf Tango Oscar Papa Golf approaching Ipswi... no, that's not right... erm... approaching... erm... a town with a large garden centre..."

"This is Golf Tango Oscar Papa Golf, now heading... sort of sideways... oh dear..."

"This is Golf Tango Oscar Papa Golf, making a turn to the east... ah, no... erm... seem to be being blown the other way, sorry..."

"Golf Tango Oscar Papa Golf to control; thanks for advice. Will proceed towards Norway... Sorry, Norwich..."

"Golf Tango Oscar Papa Golf again... I'm trying to go that way I promise, it's just the wind... oh God, I'm... erm... going backwards..."

"Say again control? King's Lynn? Errr... how on earth have I reached Scotland?"

"Golf Tango Oscar Papa Golf here... can you try not to shout at me all at the same time... thanks..."

"Maximum power... repeat, I am at maximum power... and still going backwards... Oh cock..."

"Just to confirm, control; I managed to avoid it in the end... please advise, are there any other cathedrals in the area...?"

"Golf Tango Oscar Papa Golf confirming current position... I am in some bushes... repeat, some bushes... I am near... erm... a tree."

...AND THE PROBLEMS IT CAUSED

ROYAL AIR FORCE BUSCOMBE

TRANSCRIPT EXCERPT 23/11/09

×××

GROUP CAPT. JAMES 'JOCK' MCTAVISH 506 SQD
– CONFIRM, TWO TORNADO GR4S LOST IN
COLLISION WITH EACH OTHER. OVER.

×××

FLIGHT CONTROL AIR MARSHALL PETER 'LOFTY' WYNDE-TURBYNE
– CONFIRMED. PILOTS CLAIM TO HAVE
BEEN 'DISTRACTED' BY SOMETHING. OVER.

×××

GROUP CAPT. JAMES 'JOCK' MCTAVISH 506 SQD
– BEST OF LUCK EXPLAINING THAT TO WHITEHALL. OVER.

Dear Sheik Mamkoumt

I regret to inform you that your prize mare Elegant
Sundance gave birth yesterday at 2:30pm. As I'm sure you
are aware, this is rather premature and makes it extremely
unlikely that the newborn will develop into the successful
race horse we had hoped for.

What caused such a premature birth is as yet unclear, but
we believe she may have been spooked by something,
possibly in the sky.

I can only offer my apologies for this considerable waste
of time and money.

Sincerely,

Elizabeth Catchpenny-Jones
Tall Oak Stables

Tall Oak
Stables
Frambisham, Suffolk
IP12 5RF

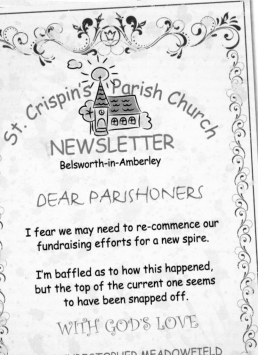

St. Crispin's Parish Church
NEWSLETTER
Belsworth-in-Amberley

DEAR PARISHONERS

I fear we may need to re-commence our
fundraising efforts for a new spire.

I'm baffled as to how this happened,
but the top of the current one seems
to have been snapped off.

WITH GOD'S LOVE

REV. CHRISTOPHER MEADOWFIELD

Bird Protection League
PO Box 5322, London N1 2FG

Bill Oddie
'Dungoodie'
London
N3 7ZV

Dear Bill,

I'm saddened to report that Britain's last mating pair of brown-headed eagles has been killed, thwarting our hopes of preventing their extinction.

Details are sketchy but our people in the East Midlands report that the eagles had become distressed, possibly as the result of a large red object in the sky which we think might have been a blimp or balloon. The sight of this craft in the breeding area, along with the loud cries of 'bollocks' emanating from it, may have startled the eagles and thus caused them to fly into the wind turbine.

I hope you're keeping well.

Jack Hampson
Director of Conservation
Bird Protection League

//DAMAGE REPORT

Overhead power lines damaged - location 45893
Overhead power lines severed - location 48336/54933

Evidence of collision with unidentified aircraft.
Traces of white fibreglass / long, possibly lady's hair on pylons

//Damage estimate: c.£26,000

www.belm.org

Archive
Guestbook
News
E-mail

The Euphasian temple of Belmology
The truth of our salvation will come from the above

Followers!!!!! The time has come at last!!!!!! After years of waiting, THE BELMOLOGICAL CRAFT IS HERE!!!!!!!!!!!!!!!!

Our EUPHASIAN brothers in the middle regions of Britain have seen the craft arrive, ready to take us all to the PROMISED LANDS OF BELMOLGIA!!!!!!!

At approximately 4 o'clock yesterday afternoon the craft did descend upon a field and hover there for some seconds making the AGREED NOISE of a small and furiously revving motor. For then was heard the AGREED CODEWORD and that word was 'COCK'.

Then did the craft make movement backwards, whereupon the AGREED CODE-PHRASE of 'OH COCKING HELL' was heard to emerge from it and lo! The craft did then decide not to land and did instead drift slowly upwards and sideways.

Our noble brothers did then make to follow the SACRED CRAFT before sadly it entered RESTRICTED AIRSPACE and was then seen DRIFTING OUT TO SEA.

FEAR NOT!!!!!!! For this is merely A SIGN that the craft is preparing us for the glorious moment when it shall finally alight 'pon this planet and the boarding process shall begin to take us to our NEW PLANET. Worry not also that the craft appears rather small for it shall be capable of making SEVERAL TRIPS to allow us to begin our NEW LIVES.

<BLINK> PLEASE REMEMBER TO PAY YOUR SUBSCRIPTIONS </BLINK>
We can't stress this enough. Cash, no cheques.

Building Services

Andy Wilman
Executive Producer, Top Gear
BBC Media Centre
201 Wood Lane
London
W12 7TS

23 July 2010

Dear Andy,

I have received yet ANOTHER request from your office to have the toner in the photocopier re-filled. In case you are not aware, this is the FIFTH such request my team has received in the last month alone.

Furthermore, in the year to date, our records show that the Top Gear office has used more than FIFTY times the average amount of toner consumed by other programmes.

I am baffled as to the cause of this abnormal and highly troubling statistic and I would welcome an explanation as to the reasons behind it.

Yours sincerely,

S. Platt

Steve Platt
Photocopier & Printer Systems Solutions Leader

HOUSE OF
MAY

Hammond HELPS

Dear Richard

Top Gear's Richard Hammond shares his car-buying wisdom

Dear Richard,
I'm a recent divorcee and for the first time in many years I need to buy a car, rather than relying on my (now ex-) husband to take care of it. I need something easy to park, economical and above all reliable. What would you recommend?
Gillian, Shrewsbury

RICHARD REPLIES...
Car buying can be an intimidating process but it doesn't need to be, as long as you go in with a very clear idea of what you want to buy. In this case, Gillian, I would advise you to buy a 1969 Chevrolet Camaro ZL1. Its 7-litre, big-block V8 engine is all aluminium rather than the usual iron and that pays dividends when it comes to weight over the front end, making it easier to park than, say, a 1970 Chevelle LS6!

Letter of the month

Dear Richard,
Since I retired two years ago, I have been quite happily running around in my old 2005 Ford Mondeo. However, the time has come to buy a new car and I'm wondering if I should simply go for another Mondeo or look at alternatives. Whatever I choose must be practical and easy to drive because I only have one arm. What would you say?
Geoff, Newbury

RICHARD REPLIES...
You're obviously a Ford man Geoff,

so I'd recommend you buy a 1967 Shelby Mustang GT350. Its 4.7-litre V8 engine is slightly smaller than that found in many other muscle cars and that makes it ideal for the retiree who needs to keep an eye on soaring fuel costs!

Dear Richard,
My 18-year-old daughter will be off to university later this year and I would like to buy her a cheap, second-hand car that will be cheap to insure and roomy enough to take all her belongings back and forth during the holidays. She only passed her test last month so it needs to be something easy to drive and, of course, it has to be safe. Any suggestions?
Roger, Harrogate

RICHARD REPLIES...
It's a question I'm often asked by proud parents and the reply I always give is the same – what you want is a 1968 Dodge Charger R/T, preferably with the 426 Hemi engine. At over 17 feet long, the Charger has a real advantage over more compact muscle cars like the Challenger when it comes to cramming in all those books, pillows, pot plants and the like!

Dear Richard,
My boyfriend has always been incredibly affectionate but

recently he started to become cold and distant. At first I was worried that it was something I had done but then last week I came home from work early and found him in a clinch with our next door neighbour. I'm absolutely devastated as we'd been talking about getting married and starting a family. I love him dearly but don't know if I can trust him again. What do I do? Please help.
Anna, Exeter

RICHARD REPLIES...
Hmmm, it sounds as if you and your boyfriend have a classic case of what we agony aunts call 'pre-commitment nerves'. I find the best thing to do in such turbulent times is to take a good long look in the mirror and say to yourself; 'Plymouth Barracuda or Pontiac GTO?' Either is good in these situations but personally, I'd opt for the classic muscle and icon looks of the GTO. But not the first version because, strictly speaking, that was just an option package for the Pontiac Tempest, as I'm sure you know!

Got a problem?
Write to:
Richard Hammond,
Take A Poo! magazine,
PO Box 433,
Grunting,
GR1 5SA

FIG 1

THE TOP GEAR PRESIDENTIAL LIMOUSINE

IN THESE DIFFICULT ECONOMIC TIMES, GOVERNMENTS AROUND THE WORLD MUST LEAD BY EXAMPLE WHEN IT COMES TO ENCOURAGING FISCAL PRUDENCE. ONE OF THE FIRST WAYS IN WHICH THEY CAN SAVE MONEY IS BY BINNING THOSE LAVISH, BULLETPROOF LIMOS THAT THEY USE TO TRANSPORT THEIR PRESIDENTS AND PREMIERS. IN THEIR PLACE THEY ARE FREE TO USE TOP GEAR'S DESIGN FOR THE BUDGET PRESIDENTIAL LIMO.

NO, REALLY, THERE'S NO NEED TO THANK US.

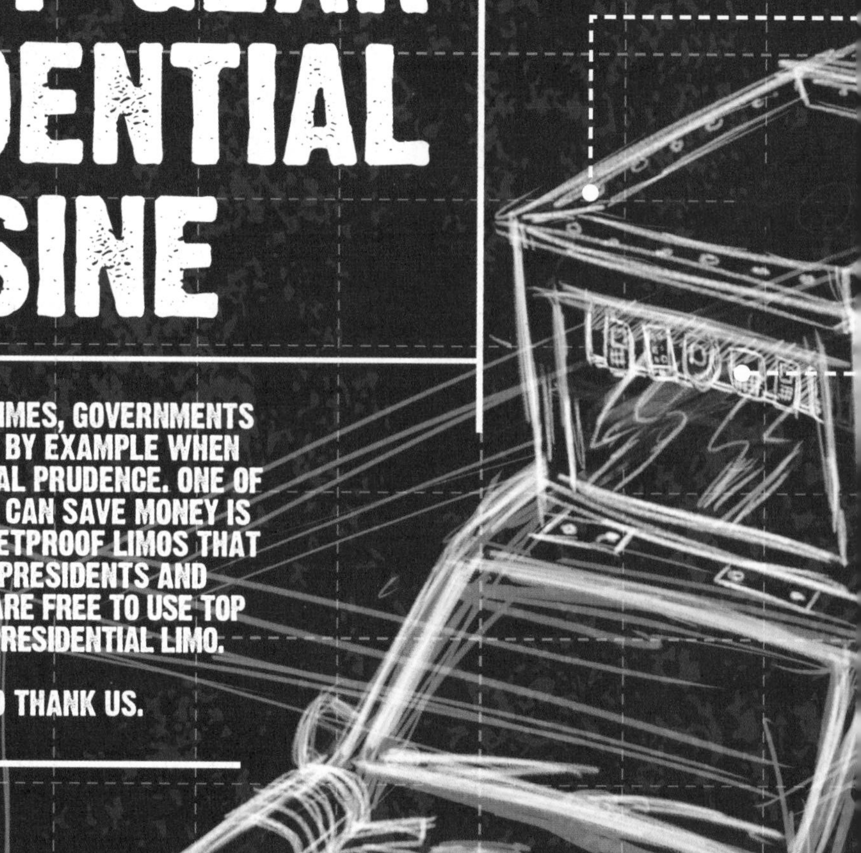

A limo needs to keep going, even when it's under attack. And nothing keeps going like a Toyota pick-up truck.

Many countries are a bit funny about guns, but the man in charge still needs protecting. That's why this limo is fitted with plastic drainpipes on the doors and on the bonnet just ahead of the windscreen. At the first sign of trouble the driver and passenger can drop fireworks into these tubes and they will launch towards the threat, scaring it off.

Some high-ranking politicians favour cars with run-flat tyres so they can drive off, even under a hail of bullets. But run-flat tyres are quite expensive so the TG 'limo' uses a cheaper and far more ingenious solution. Normal tyres, filled with jelly. In this case raspberry. But any flavour will do.

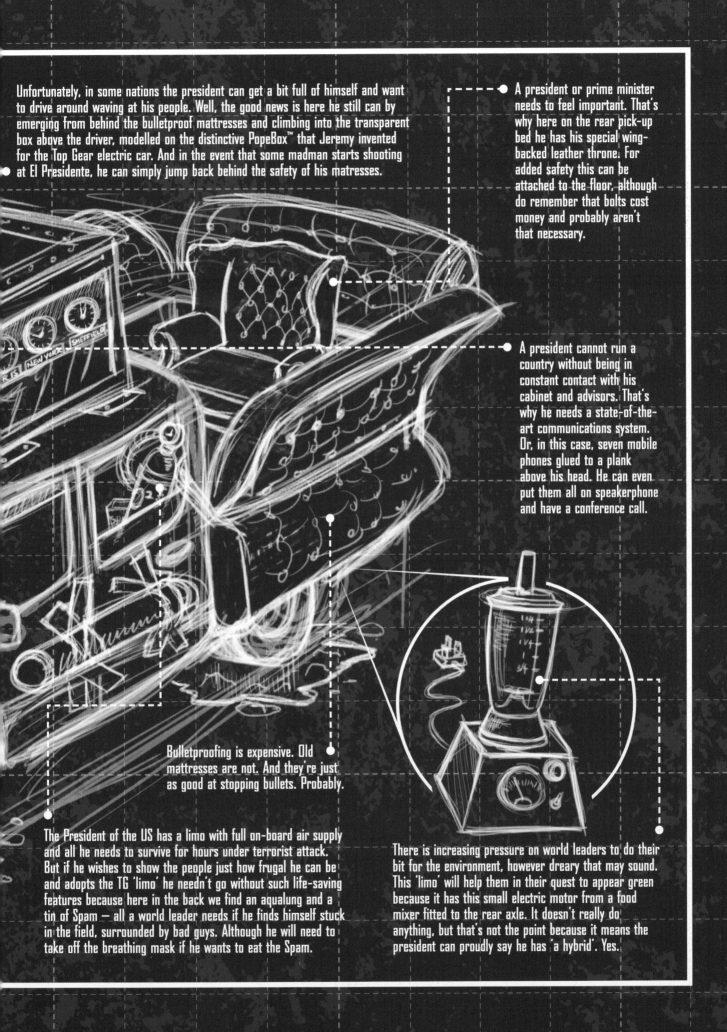

Unfortunately, in some nations the president can get a bit full of himself and want to drive around waving at his people. Well, the good news is here he still can by emerging from behind the bulletproof mattresses and climbing into the transparent box above the driver, modelled on the distinctive PopeBox™ that Jeremy invented for the Top Gear electric car. And in the event that some madman starts shooting at El Presidente, he can simply jump back behind the safety of his mattresses.

A president or prime minister needs to feel important. That's why here on the rear pick-up bed he has his special wing-backed leather throne. For added safety this can be attached to the floor, although do remember that bolts cost money and probably aren't that necessary.

A president cannot run a country without being in constant contact with his cabinet and advisors. That's why he needs a state-of-the-art communications system. Or, in this case, seven mobile phones glued to a plank above his head. He can even put them all on speakerphone and have a conference call.

Bulletproofing is expensive. Old mattresses are not. And they're just as good at stopping bullets. Probably.

The President of the US has a limo with full on-board air supply and all he needs to survive for hours under terrorist attack. But if he wishes to show the people just how frugal he can be and adopts the TG 'limo' he needn't go without such life-saving features because here in the back we find an aqualung and a tin of Spam — all a world leader needs if he finds himself stuck in the field, surrounded by bad guys. Although he will need to take off the breathing mask if he wants to eat the Spam.

There is increasing pressure on world leaders to do their bit for the environment, however dreary that may sound. This 'limo' will help them in their quest to appear green because it has this small electric motor from a food mixer fitted to the rear axle. It doesn't really do anything, but that's not the point because it means the president can proudly say he has 'a hybrid'. Yes.

THE PACIFIC ISLAND OF OOM

The island of Oom might be considered by some as just another part of the Kalonesia sub-region of the South Pacific but it is, in many ways, unique. With a population of just 2000, this tiny colony adrift in a vast ocean is a land very much apart from the rest of the world, with its own rudimentary government, its own recognized currency and centuries of unique customs. What really makes Oom unique, however, is that its inhabitants have access to just one television, capable of receiving just a single, intermittent feed from the UK-based TV channel, Dave. As a result, most Oomians have seen only one programme in their entire lives – the popular BBC motoring show, *Top Gear*. Furthermore, due to the flickering vagaries of their satellite signal, the people of this isolated land are under the mistaken impression that it is a fly-on-the-wall documentary.

It is Thursday night in Moonja, the main settlement on Oom. As night draws in, excitable Oomians dash along the tracks and trails between the simple huts that make up this small town, all rushing towards the large clearing in front of the High Ruler's residence, for it is here that the country's one television will be brought forth and, pending clear skies and a constant flow of power from the nearby wind turbine, a flickering picture will appear on its screen. It is time for what the locals call *The Silly Man And He Friends*.

The people of Oom speak their own language, a unique Kalonesian dialect known as Oomish, but as the programme progresses the High Ruler, a well-known Anglophile who lived for four years in Ipswich, provides a running commentary so his people can keep abreast of what is happening on screen.

'The High Ruler is explaining that the silly men are now going on holiday,' says our translator. 'But they have missed the ferry, probably because of the Silly Man With Much Hair, and they have had to build their own boats to reach a distant land. This must surely remind us of the time that The Silly Man Who Is Small and the Silly Man With Much Hair wished to visit some friends in outer space and attempted to fashion the curious white craft that failed with much fury and was followed by the Silly Man Who Is Noisy laughing with great joy.'

On the fuzzy TV screen, the *Top Gear* presenters are now engaged in the familiar news segment of the show. Our translator, however, makes it clear that the High Ruler sees this segment differently. 'The Ruler, he says that the silly men have now returned to their house,' he says slowly. 'And that, as usual, they have many guests in the house, so many that there are not enough chairs to sit down. But we should not worry, for later one of the guests will be permitted to sit down whilst the Silly Man Who Is Small and the Silly Man With Much Hair are gone, and the Silly Man Who Is Noisy will be most polite and ask this person many questions about a book or film that they have taken part in.'

It is quite extraordinary to see the interest that this flickering, barely visible television programme inspires in the people of Oom. I ask our translator if the show brings joy to the islanders. 'Yes, we enjoy to see how the silly men are doing,' he says. 'But also we worry for them. Too often they are involved in the accidents, such as recently when the Silly Man Who Is Noisy did try to drive to see his friends and his car was only with the three wheels and he did fall over many times and into a river. Also, we worry about the Silly Man Who Is Small. Can I ask you, what on earth has he done to his hair?'

> **"It is quite extraordinary to see the interest that this flickering, barely visible television programme inspires in the people of Oom."**

Effigies of the Silly Man Who Is Noisy And Has Funny Hair appear all over the island

HOW WELL DO YOU KNOW...

Richard Hammond

With his boyish good looks and extensive collection of barely functioning old Land Rovers, who wouldn't be a fan of Richard Hammond? But how much do you actually know about him?

1. Richard likes to play what with his bass guitar?
a. Stinky hot funk ❑
b. Silky moist jazz ❑
c. Rounders ❑

2. During his radio career, what was Richard's DJ name?
a. Night Weasel ❑
b. The Duke of Westminster ❑
c. Janice Long ❑

3. Which one of these programmes did Richard NOT present?
a. When Trees Fall Over ❑
b. All Dentist Ultimate Smackdown ❑
c. Massive Horses ❑

4. Richard lives in which Herefordshire town?
a. Cheese-on-Toast ❑
b. Irony-upon-Irony ❑
c. Screaming-in-Agony ❑

5. Which one of these British sports cars does Richard NOT own?
a. Morgan Aeromintchocolate ❑
b. Morgan Aerobicsclass ❑
c. Morgan Aeropuerto del Generalissimo Morello ❑

6. Richard has recently learned to fly what?
a. Off the handle ❑
b. Out of a cannon ❑
c. Unaided ❑

Answers

1. Runny cheese 2. The Lancashire Hotpot 3. Britain's Funniest Appendectomies 4. Bumhole 5. Morgan Freeman 6. Spray

Are you a JAAAG driver?

We've all fancied a Jaguar at some point in our lives, but being a true Jaaaag driver takes more than simply buying an old XJ or XJS off eBay. Find out if you're cut out for a charming but disreputable life with a charming but disreputable car by taking this simple quiz.

You've taken a lady out for dinner. What sort of conversation would you make during the meal?

A) Polite small talk, studiously avoiding controversial topics such as religion and politics

B) A series of well-rehearsed anecdotes carefully designed to entertain and amuse

C) Outrageous flirting... with the waitress serving you

At the end of the meal, how would you pay?

A) Cash

B) Credit card

C) Ah... I seem to have left my wallet in the Jaaaag. Would you mind awfully helping me out on this one..?

When letting a lady into your Jaaaag, what would you do?

A) Allow her to get in herself. This is the 21st century, after all

B) Open the passenger door for her. Manners cost nothing, remember

C) Open the passenger door for her... so you can catch a glimpse up her skirt as she gets in

When do you file your tax returns?

A) As soon as the financial year is over

B) On the latest possible date without incurring penalty

C) Ah, if that's the taxman on the phone would you mind awfully telling him I'm in Belize again. Missing. Probably dead

Some money mysteriously appears in your bank account. What would you do?

A) Call the police

B) Call the bank

C) Money? I don't recall any money, old chum

A friend asks you to look after his collection of vintage watches whilst he is away on business for six months. Where would you store them?

A) In a safe

B) Under the bed, carefully hidden in a suitcase

C) Your watches? Well the damndest thing. A jackdaw stole them. Yes, all eight of them. Blasted scavenger probably sold them to a watch dealer in Chichester... erm, I would imagine

Where would you park your car at night?

A) In the garage next to your house

B) In the car park underneath your apartment building

C) Outside the flat you used to live in until that slight... *misunderstanding* with the mortgage company

Where did you get that jacket from?

A) Marks & Spencer

B) Gieves & Hawkes

C) Oh gosh, is this yours? I do apologize. I must have picked it up by accident when I was at your house. When was I at your house? Ah, well you see you dropped your house keys in my Jaaaaaaag and when I popped by to return them, well you weren't actually there. So I just sort of let myself in. Your dog? Missing? Ah...

TWF 593H

THE DOCKLAND HOTEL
Freighter Way, Belfast

Nice hotel. Spoilt only by lack of crane to get my car out of the dock. Also, don't bother holding Mr Kemp's room. He's not coming back.

Jeremy Clarkson

HOTEL SPLENDIDIO
2012 Placa del Dust, La Paz, Bolivia

Name / Nombre: Richard Hammond

Place of residence / Domicilio: Britain

The hotel / El hotel
- ❏ Excellent / Excellente
- ❏ Average / Medio
- ❏ Poor / Malo
- ☑ Air too thin, funny smell / Aero mucho thinos, smello del noto niceo

Your room / Su dormitorio
- ❏ Excellent / Excellente
- ❏ Average / Medio
- ❏ Poor / Malo
- ☑ Full of insects / fullo del animales irritatio

The food / El alimento
- ❏ Excellent / Excellente
- ❏ Average / Medio
- ❏ Poor / Malo
- ☑ Bits in it / Errrr

THE SCRAPMAN'S ARMS
19 SHITELY ROAD, BIRMINGHAM, B42 6FH

Very pleasant stay in this beautiful part of England. Particularly enjoyed the magnificent views of the Elizabethan railway shunting yard and the Rococo splendour of the industrial plastics recycling facility. Surprised and delighted to find my TVR S2 still parked outside in the morning.

James May, London

THE BORO HOTEL
234 SMOGGY STREET, MIDDLESBROUGH, TS1 4RE

Name - Richard Hammond

Message - Come and see our art exhibition.
Come and see our art exhibition. Come and see our art exhibition.
Come and see our art exhibition. Come and see our art exhibition.
Come and see our art exhibition. Come and see our art exhibition.

John Hanway and family, Telford
Lovely hotel, relaxing time here in the North East spoilt only by going to
see the Top Gear art exhibition which was confusing and awful.

EL BURRO DE LA TORRE DE IGLESIA

Placa Del Tortura Animale, Majorca, 5432

Disappointing. Your dining room
was unable to supply a high chair
for one of my colleagues. Nor his
dwarf co-driver. Ha ha ha.

Jeremy Clarkson

THE SNAKE'S BLOOD INN
Ha Long, Vietnam

I can only apologize
for the amount of sea
water I seem to have
got on your carpets.
Also, there may be
some bits of statue
jammed in the
plughole of the bath.
Sorry.

James May, London

THE ONLY FOUR THINGS IN THE WORLD THAT ALL THREE TOP GEAR PRESENTERS ACTUALLY AGREE ON...

1 THE RANGE ROVER

It's a living legend and it makes you feel special every time you drive one. Plus, as *Top Gear*'s camera tracking car of choice, the show couldn't be made without it.

2 THE FORD MONDEO

It's comfortable, practical, sensibly priced and well equipped. It even looks quite nice. Basically, it's just about everything you'll ever need from a car.

3 THE SUBARU LEGACY OUTBACK

It's nice to drive and it has real personality, plus it's somehow able to blend seamlessly into any situation from supermarket car park to manor house driveway.

4 SANDWICH SPREAD

It's yummy and it has... oh wait, apparently only Jeremy and James like sandwich spread. Richard thinks it's disgusting. Sorry.

Hot Hatches

They killed the British sports car in the '80s, but we still love 'em

VW GOLF GTI

This is the real genesis of the hot hatchback. The original. The daddy. And yet, strangely, Volkswagen had no plans for a Golf GTI at all. This car was the result of a team of engineers playing around in their spare time, coming up with what they originally called the 'Sport Golf' and doing it completely under the radar until such a time as it was ready. Even then, management weren't convinced and cautiously signed off a limited run of what they renamed the GTI. We're glad they did. None more so than Jeremy, who admired it so much that he can still reel off a vast list of geek-tastic stats about it.

PEUGEOT 205 GTI

If the Golf GTI is the father of hot hatches, this is the prodigal son. It's also the car that finally smashed to pieces Peugeot's previous image as a builder of boring saloons, taking as it did the pretty 205 hatch and fitting it with a lively, lumpy brat of an engine that gave the GTI the feeling that it was, at any moment, about to burst apart at the seams. This impression was cemented by all the bits of trim that would fall off the car during your ownership, but truth is the basic structure was strong and when you were having that much fun driving it, you really didn't care about anything else.

FIAT STRADA ABARTH

The Strada Abarth wasn't the best hot hatchback of the 1980s. It certainly wasn't the most popular. It was rattly, it was tinny, it had strange wind deflectors above the side windows, and front seats that didn't tilt forward properly to let people into the back. There was, in other words, much that was wrong with it. But when that tuneful twin-carb, twin-cam, two-litre engine came on song you'd soon realize what was right with it too. The Abarth certainly wasn't one of the better-remembered hatchbacks of the '80s but it was probably one of the most fun and undoubtedly one of the most mental.

RENAULT CLIO WILLIAMS

Its name might have sounded like a 1950s jazz singer, but the Clio Williams was *the* benchmark small hot hatch of the 1990s. Like the Peugeot 205 GTI before it, the Clio used the simple formula of light, tinny, shopping-car body melded to oversized saloon-car engine and the net result was lots of fun. It worked out so well that the Williams – named after the F1 team of the same name – set the template for the superb fast Renaults we have today. The only flaw at the time was that it was called a limited edition... until Renault made a load more, rather annoying owners of the originals.

LANCIA DELTA INTEGRALE

It wasn't a pretty car. It wasn't blessed with an attractive interior. It would probably start to rattle soon after you bought it. But in almost every other respect, the Delta Integrale was so wonderful that owners would probably rather sell their children than have to sell the car. The Integrale was a proper live wire, fast in a straight line and – thanks to its four-wheel drive system – even faster round corners, which was no surprise since its real purpose was to win rallies. Which, by the way, it did, bagging the World Rally Championship for an incredible *five* years in a row.

FORD ESCORT COSWORTH

Like the Lancia, the Escort RS Cosworth – or 'Cos-eh' – was a happy spin-off from Ford's involvement in rallying. In this case, the Escort wasn't an Escort but the mechanical bits of the Sierra Cosworth 4x4 stuffed into an Escort shell. All the wider arches, vents and wings were created by a design agency who got the job after Ford was impressed with the neat work they'd done on styling the Escort van. The same company later worked on a proposal for a small Aston based on the Cosworth chassis. Sadly, Ford vetoed it in favour of the Jag-based DB7, denying the world a really pretty Cos-eh.

THE TOP GEAR TAPESTRY

This extraordinary woven cloth artwork, recently discovered in a skip near Guildford, leads experts to believe that the world's most popular car show has been around for longer than originally thought

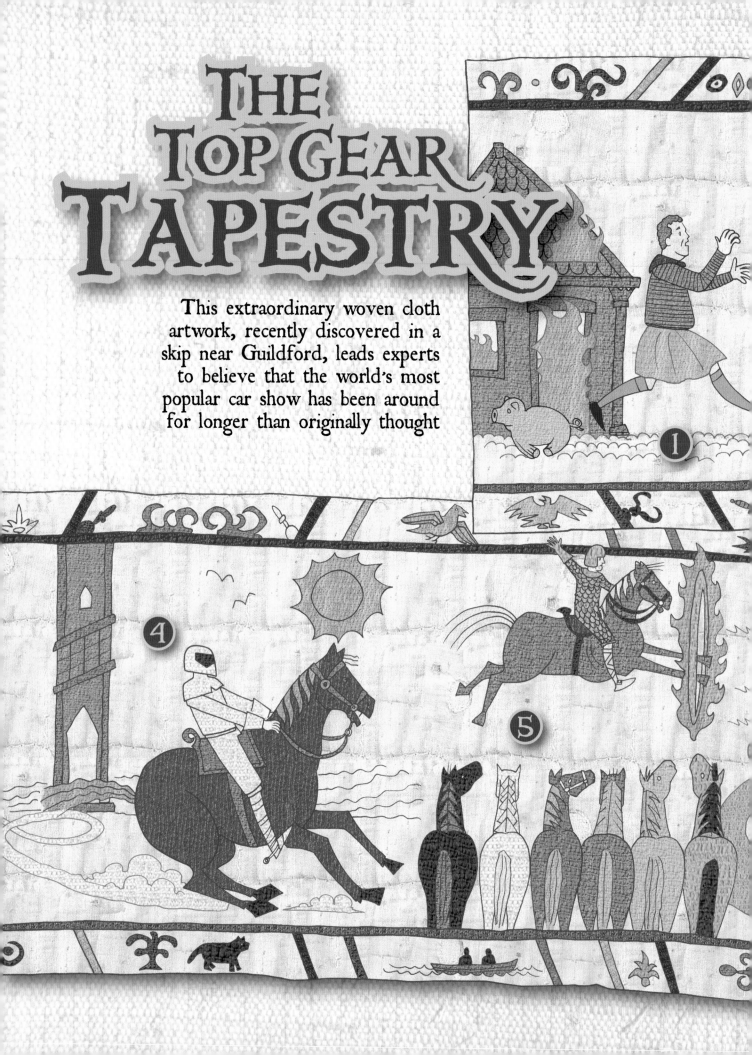

POTS

YE TEUTONIC SPORTY HORSE

① Here we see Lord Clarkson of Shouting, the famously impractical nobleman much referred to in contemporary texts as 'Ye frizzie haiyred idiote', who appears to have accidentally set fire to someone else's house.

② Captured here in fascinating detail is Lord Hammond of Whitening who has accepted thirty pieces of silver in return for making what was known at the time as a 'personyl appearyance'. It is believed that the dashing nobleman would have accepted his payment for he was keen to buy yet another of 'ye Teutonic sportie horse' from the premises next door.

③ In this part of the tapestry we see Sir Jaymes May positing his radical theory that the earth revolves around the sun, rather than the other way around. Although his brave scientific endeavours have attracted a crowd, this crowd has fallen into a deep sleep, a curious phenomenon explained by a contemporary text which recorded that 'Sir Jaymes did goe into too much detaile and t'was most boringe'.

④ This tapestry is the first known record of a curious character referred to in subsequent texts as 'Ye Styg'. Little is known about this mysterious figure, save that he was said to be capable of 'making an horse travel at speeds that yon eyes would scaryce believe' and that he 'did sleep upsydown 'pon a tree, lyke a massyve bat'.

⑤ Historians have argued for many years over the significance of this scene but it is broadly agreed to depict a character known as 'Top Geare Stuyntmann'. This figure is mentioned just once in a journal from the time and referred to as 'a most shyte idea that was dropp'd after just one seryes'.

⑥ This figure is considered to be Lord Jaye of Kaye leaning on what many believe is 'Ye Horse Of Most Reesonyble Pryce'. Recently discovered documents suggest that Lord Kaye had 'jyst sette ye fastest lappe and was verily driven to perform a most hilaryous dance'. The figure in the background is thought to be King Simon X, also known as The Highe Trousyre King, who was said to be 'most furious to have his lappe tyme beaten and the smugge smyle wyped from his fayce'.

SPÉĂK ROMĂNIĂN

If you're an international traveller, you can often find yourself in a bit of a tight spot when Mr Jonathan Foreigner refuses to speak the Queen's English. But worry not, because TV's James May is here to help with his seamless grasp of many foreign languages including, as he demonstrated during a *Top Gear* trip to Eastern Europe, the tricky mother tongue of Romania. Here are some of the phrases he would advise you to use if you find yourself in a convertible supercar on an epic journey to find the world's greatest road.

ENGLISH	RÔMĂŅÎĂŅ
Is there a hotel near here?	Čăŋ yôü şüpply mé wîţh qüâŋţîţîéş öf yéăşţ?
Do you have a room for the night?	Wôüld yôü lîké mé ţô ţôüčh yôür făčé?
I would like to check out please.	Î hăvé čréăţéd ă ţrüly ăwfül şméll.
I would like to reserve a table for three people.	Îţ îş ŋôţ wîdély kŋôwŋ ţhăţ Î öwŋ şévéŋ wéăşélş.
Do you have a wine list?	Whéŋ wîll yôü réléăşé wăşpş îŋţö my făčé?
Could I have the bill please?	Why dö yôü hăvé pîčţüréş ôf my şîşţér?
Is the town hall near here?	Whăţ şôrţ ôf čréşş dö yôü şéll?
I am looking for the centre of the town.	Î hăvé réčéŋţly pürčhăşéd ă ğréăţ déâl ôf dôüblé ğlăşîŋğ.
I am looking for a petrol station.	Î ăm ğôîŋğ ţô şţéăl âll yôür shélvéş.
Do you take credit cards?	Whăţ thé héll îş ăll ţhîş ğrééŋ şţüff?

IN CONVERSATION

>> **FINCHLEY HIGHGATE** asks two of the stars of the BBC's Top Gear programme how they would tackle public transport for the future.

James May: Public transport? Hmm, I'm glad you've asked me that…

Richard Hammond: Can I just point out that within 20 minutes or so, you won't be glad you asked him that.

James May: No, but it's an interesting one isn't it. I was thinking about this the other day and, well it's something I've believed for a while actually, that if you look at railways, the impressive thing about them isn't the trains or the way the networks currently operate, it's the civil engineering behind them, the bridges and the tunnels and so forth…

Richard Hammond: Oh God.

James May: And the tunnels in particular gave me an idea. I mean, if you think about, say, the London Underground, the actual amount of the network that has a train on it at any given point is very small. In other words, there are vast lengths of tunnel that are empty. That's just a necessity of safety and scheduling and what have you.

Richard Hammond: What are you on about?

James May: Hang on, hang on, I'm getting to that. My point is that all this tunnelling being empty starts to feel a bit, well, inefficient. And so I've had an idea…

Richard Hammond: Of course you have.

James May: …and it applies not just to the Tube in London but to anywhere with an underground; Paris, New York, Newcastle, wherever you like. First of all, you've got to get rid of the trains…

Richard Hammond: You think underground train networks should get rid of the trains?

James May: Yes, get rid of the trains and make the tunnels into a highway network for scooters.

Richard Hammond: A what? A highway network for scooters? How's that going to work?

James May: You just need to put in a floor, just above where the rails were, and then people can ride scooters around until they get where they want to go in the city.

Richard Hammond: And then they have to lug a scooter up an escalator.

James May: No, the scooters stay underground. You pay to use them.

Richard Hammond: This is honestly the worst idea I've ever heard. Everyone would just crash into each other.

James May: But why would that happen? They don't crash into each other on the road.

Richard Hammond: Because on the road they're not crammed together, in a tunnel, IN THE DARK.

James May: You're being obtuse. It's perfectly easy to ride in a straight line and obviously I'd light the tunnels. Or the scooters.

Richard Hammond: And would you provide helmets for all the people who are going to be involved in this enormous underground scooter accident?

James May: Well this is the bit that worries me actually, because there could be quite a lot of logistics involved in maintaining the scooters, hiring them out, providing helmets and so on…

Richard Hammond: You don't say?

James May: So I've been thinking about an parallel plan.

Richard Hammond: Unicycles? No wait, bears. Bears that carry you through the darkness in complete comfort and safety.

James May: Don't be fatuous. The thought I had, and I hope readers of Global Transport Solutions will appreciate this more than my colleague here, is to have scooters in one tunnel and in the other, to introduce waterways so people could go by boat around under the city…

Richard Hammond: Yes James, that's a brilliant idea. Really brilliant. I bet there's lots of people just sitting around thinking, I personally don't find using this underground train at all frightening. If only these tunnels had been flooded and then filled with lots of scooters that could smash into each in the pitch darkness whilst we're all attacked by bears…

James May: I never said anything about bears, that was you.

"You just put in a floor and people can ride scooters around until they get where they want to go in the city"

Richard Hammond: Actually, can I distance myself from this whole thing. Don't put my name on it. Call me Bronco Cockhat or something.

James May: I'm telling you, this is a very workable idea.

Bronco Cockhat: Kill me. Kill me now.

NEXT WEEK: TRAFFIC MANAGEMENT AND MAJOR CONURBATION PLANNING WITH VERNON KAYE AND TESS DALY

THE TOP GEAR PERSONALIZED NUMBER PLATE DE-CODING SOLUTION SYSTEM SOLUTION

816 MAN

WHAT IT'S SUPPOSED TO SAY:
BIG MAN

WHAT IT REALLY SAYS:
TWOT

WHAT IT'S SUPPOSED TO SAY:
POSH GIRL

WHAT IT REALLY SAYS:
BERK

PO54 GRL

G33 ZER

WHAT IT'S SUPPOSED TO SAY:
GEEZER

WHAT IT REALLY SAYS:
WAZZOCK

WHAT IT'S SUPPOSED TO SAY:
KITTEN

WHAT IT REALLY SAYS:
CLEFT

K17 TEN

RU01 GBY

WHAT IT'S SUPPOSED TO SAY:
RUGBY

WHAT IT REALLY SAYS:
DIVVY

WHAT IT'S SUPPOSED TO SAY:
JESUS

WHAT IT REALLY SAYS:
ERM, ACTUALLY LET'S JUST
LEAVE THIS ONE ALONE.

J3 SUS

HOW WELL DO YOU KNOW...

Jeremy Clarkson

Everyone's a fan of *Top Gear*'s Jeremy Clarkson. Except Piers Morgan. And he's an arse. But how well do you actually know the pube-headed tall one off *Top Gear*?

1. Jeremy's first magazine journalism job was for who?
a. Uncompromising Campanologist Monthly ❑
b. Mobile Arsonist Weekly ❑
c. Exaggeration Literally Every Second ❑

2. Jeremy is allergic to what?
a. Butters ❑
b. Running ❑
c. E.M. Forster ❑

3. Jeremy buys all his shoes from where?
a. Tramps ❑
b. Tamworth ❑
c. TV Times ❑

4. Before joining *Top Gear*, Jeremy was best known for owning what?
a. Britain's fourth largest collection of ABBA memorabilia ❑
b. Britain's second most interesting crow ❑
c. Wiltshire ❑

5. Which of these things has Jeremy never done?
a. Used the word 'text' as a verb ❑
b. Knowingly spoken to someone from Winchester ❑
c. Assassinated the serving prime minister of a Benelux nation ❑

6. How many chairs did Jeremy recently claim to own?
a. None ❑
b. Seven ❑
c. Too many ❑

Answers

IF TOP GEAR BUILT...

The world would be a rather different place if Jeremy, Richard and James were the chief engineers.

Look, as far as I'm concerned this is near enough.

Well, is there a drawing on the box we could copy?

TOP GEAR CHALLENGE

BOLIVIA

WHEN TOP GEAR WENT TO BOTSWANA, THEY SUCCESSFULLY PROVED THAT YOU DON'T NEED A FOUR-WHEEL-DRIVE CAR TO GET ACROSS CHALLENGING TERRAIN. SO, THE ONLY LOGICAL WAY TO MOVE ON FROM THAT WAS TO TRAVEL TO SOUTH AMERICA AND PROVE THAT, ACTUALLY, SOMETIMES YOU DO

TOP GEAR CHALLENGE

1 May, Clarkson and Hammond start their journey on a creaking motorboat. Though apparently built from lolly sticks and optimism, this would prove the most reliable mode of transport they would encounter in South America.

2 Our trio of intrepid adventurers meet their internet-bought cars for the first time. Thankfully, they are exactly as they were described in the adverts. In everything but colour, engine, age, odour and workingness.

4 This is Richard, making blistering progress through the tough Bolivian undergrowth. Or possibly sinking helplessly into an anaconda-infested swamp. In fact, it's almost definitely the latter.

3 Survival experts say these supplies are vital for jungle driving. And that a Rampant Rabbit will sterilize 14 litres of river water. Hmmm.

5 'Dear The Bolivian Trading Standards Authority. Having recently purchased a car from a reputable classifieds website, I was shocked to find it did not meet the description. The advert clearly failed to list the giant snake in the engine bay...'

6 Richard listens intently to Jeremy's tips for staying hydrated in humid climes. Jeremy is holding aloft his Pointing Finger Of Gross Misinformation.

I'M GONNA CUT YOU SOME NEW AIR VENTS

7 Jeremy demonstrates to the locals all of the ingenuity, dexterity and inventiveness that make British automotive engineers the envy of the world. Stunned by his wizardry, the locals kindly ask Jeremy to leave their country immediately and never return.

TOP GEAR CHALLENGE

9 After several weeks without washing, some say your body begins to 'self-clean', eventually leaving you perfectly odourless and sanitary. Richard has not reached this stage. He smells of long-deceased cat.

8 From page 125 of Richard's *Massive Book Of Nasty Poisonous Things That Want You Dead*, it's... the Sabre-Toothed Tree Badger! No, hang on...

10 Look! At last! A proper road! Well, a dirt track, at least. A dirt track most likely built to aid large-scale narcotics trafficking, true, but every cloud has a silver lining – and we are that choking, dusty silver lining. Cough. Splutter.

11 Several Bolivians mistakenly believed James to be Jesus himself, returned from 40 days in the wilderness. Then they smelt his T-shirt and lost all faith in a benign God.

13 Parallel parking, as endorsed by the Bolivian School of Motoring. Notice efficient use of space and unhappy Brummie trapped in the foliage.

12 The boys cross a bridge into the unknown. Actually, it's a bridge into a small Bolivian town that makes wooden carvings of capybaras, but that doesn't sound so epic.

14 Jeremy encouters a Large Car on the Death Road. Thankfully, the Range Rover is renowned for its narrow proportions and cat-like reflexes. Hence JC's relaxed expression and total lack of stainage in the trouser region.

HOLY **COW**, THIS ROAD'S **DEADLY**

15 Jeremy peruses his Haynes manual for 'Common Range Rover problems that can be easily fixed with hammers, fire and shouting'.

RANGE ROVER

16 Jeremy and Richard pick up supplies in the Altiplana's world-renowned Booze, Nudey Girls'n'Illicit Substances Emporium. Now open on Sundays, Bank Holidays and Festivals of the Virgin!

18 Addled by the dangerously thin air, Jeremy desperately digs in the dirt for oxygen.

BIENVENIDO A CHILE

17 'Welcome to Chile', says the sign. 'Bet this sounded like a top idea in the pub a few months ago, right?' says the writing below. Spanish is a pithy language.

20 Jeremy celebrates in magnanimous fashion. James's hair concedes defeat.

19 Richard's Land Cruiser plunges to an untimely death. And by 'untimely' we mean 'long overdue and probably best for all concerned'.

THE LAST GALLON OF PETROL

If you had the world's last gallon of petrol, what would you do with it? Here are a few of your options

Drive a Bugatti Veyron flat out for just under a minute [1]

Take a supercharged Range Rover for one last 12.5-mile trip [2]

Go from Oxford to Southampton in a Toyota iQ [3]

Ride 52 miles on a Suzuki Hayabusa [4]

Fly James' Super Decathlon aeroplane for just over seven minutes [5]

Drive a ride-on lawn mower for about an hour and a half [6]

Play with a petrol-powered remote-control car for 10 hours [7]

Drink it [8]

[1] At maximum speed, a Veyron uses 1.16 gallons of fuel per minute

[2] Range Rover Autobiography V8 Supercharged; official urban fuel consumption figure =12.5mpg

[3] Distance from Oxford to Southampton = 66 miles. Toyota iQ 1.0 VVT-i, official combined economy figure = 65.7mpg

[4] Suzuki Hayabusa GSX1300R official 'highway' economy figure = 52mpg

[5] Based on James' calculation that his aeroplane uses approximately 8.33 gallons per hour during level flight

[6] Based on Kawasaki-engined ride-on mower using approximately 0.6 gallons per hour

[7] Super Chief petrol-powered remote-control car with 0.1-gallon petrol tank claimed to last for one hour

[8] Because life without petrol probably isn't worth living

THE RICHARD HAMMOND HOLIDAY DESTINATION SELECTION ASSISTANCE SYSTEM

Choosing where to go on holiday can be tricky. But with *Top Gear*'s British holiday enthusiast Richard Hammond and his handy holiday decision chart solution system, picking the place to go for your next break should be a piece of cake.*

BRITAIN

FOOD
Nice, not too fancy.

DRINK
Brown, warm.

WEATHER
Bracing and drizzly.

ROADSIGNS
Easily understood.

PEOPLE
Friendly.

LODGING
Camping. Lovely.

TRAVEL
Car. To the Lake District.

ENTERTAINMENT
Scrabble and long walks.

CLOTHES
Warm coats, jumpers.

LANGUAGE
English.

ABROAD

FOOD
Got bits in, foreign.

DRINK
Fizzy, foreign.

WEATHER
Sweaty and foreign.

ROADSIGNS
Stupidly foreign.

PEOPLE
Speak foreign.

LODGING
Full of insects. Foreign.

TRAVEL
Aeroplane. To somewhere foreign.

ENTERTAINMENT
Noisy and foreign things.

CLOTHES
Vests, foreign hats.

LANGUAGE
Foreign.

*Delicious buttered fruit cake, not that weird foreign stuff with grapes in it or something.

BBC

Accounts Department

To: The Head of Programmes

17 June 2010

Dear Deborah,

As you know, the BBC is currently looking to make significant savings across all areas of the organization.

To this end, I have come up with a rather nifty scheme to merge key programmes, starting with a union between *Blue Peter* and *Top Gear*.

The synergies between these two shows are obvious: they both have three presenters; they both make silly things out of old rubbish; they're both enjoyed by adults even though they're basically rather childish. In fact, this match is so perfect I don't know why we didn't think of it before!

Here's to the future of *Blue Top Peter Gear*!

All the best,

S. Turonnies

Simon Turonnies
BBC Senior Accountant

Those Great Lancias in Full

LANCIA GAMMA COUPE

Yes, it would rust like a sunken trawler and yes, you could lunch the entire engine simply by using full steering lock on a cold morning, but come on... just look at it!

LANCIA APRILLIA

Yes, it was weirdly only made in right-hand drive when most of Europe sat on the left and yes, its clever pillarless doors left a gap for the weather to get in, but come on... just look at it!

LANCIA MONTE CARLO

Yes, the floor could rot through until you felt like Fred Flintstone and yes, the brakes were either lethally powerful (early cars) or lethally useless (later cars), but come on... just look at it!

Yes, the pedals were inexplicably on the passenger side and yes, the short wheelbase would make it spin at the merest provocation, but come on... just look at it!

LANCIA 037

Yes, it was impossibly hot and noisy and yes, it soldiered on in rallying with just a pair of driven wheels when everyone else had gone to four-wheel drive, but come on... just look at it!

LANCIA FULVIA HF

Yes, it could be fragile as an egg shell and yes, it was ridiculously expensive when new, but come on... just look at it!

LANCIA DELTA INTEGRALE

Yes, it looked like a pile of cardboard boxes and yes, the interior was about as stylish as a cagoule, but come on... just drive it! That's right, this was the exception that proved the rule.

7400-K--001-AA-BB-DB-35
7400DT.PPD (00:00:AA:45)
00-00-11---F372-000:>00

HOUSE OF
STIG

IMDB
The Inaccurate Movie Database

Search [_____] **Go**

Movies ▾ **TV** ▾ **News** ▾ **Video** ▾ **Community** ▾

Pride & Extreme Prejudice (2008)
Director: Jeremy Clarkson
Plot: As Lizzie and Mr Darcy settle down to spend the rest of their lives together, their cosy Georgian world is interrupted by the curious arrival of a McDonnell Douglas F-15 Eagle containing chisel-jawed, snake-trousered, international spy Troy Thrusthammer who immediately cleaves their world in two… literally, using a gas axe and several machine guns. Soon the Bennet sisters realize their lives will never be the same again. Because they are all pregnant.
Genre: Excessive action **User Rating:** ★⯨☆☆☆☆☆☆☆☆

The Remains Of The Day 2 (2004)
Director: Jeremy Clarkson
Plot: A repressed and socially hamstrung butler continues to shake off the shackles of pre-war mores thanks to his burgeoning relationship with the fair Miss Kenton until suddenly she is killed by an air strike from a band of evil Nazi death troopers. The butler vows revenge and tools up with hand guns, grenades and rocket launchers before setting off around the world to avenge the death of his loved one, leading to a thrilling finale on the moon.
Genre: Silly **User Rating:** ★★⯨☆☆☆☆☆☆☆

Bridget Jones – Mission To Mars (2010)
Director: Jeremy Clarkson
Plot: In this third film, Bridget Jones has decided to stop mooning about the place worrying about relationships and has suddenly become a sexy international spy who unearths information through her job as a lap dancer, played by Megan Fox. When one of her clients dies by exploding in slow motion, Bridget decides to investigate further and unearths a web of international deceit and intrigue that eventually leads her to the Red Planet itself. In a bikini.
Genre: Inexplicable **User Rating:** ★⯨☆☆☆☆☆☆☆☆

Another Room With A View (2009)
Director: Jeremy Clarkson
Plot: Lucy Honeychurch is now happily married to George Emerson and the pair of them live a happy life in the Britain of 1911. Except that neither of them realize they are actually both spies working to stop the Russians buying British plans for a top-secret stealth fighter until a chance car chase brings them together and from then on they vow to fight the enemies together in locations as far flung as Egypt, the Bahamas and outer space.
Genre: Ludicrous **User Rating:** ★★⯨☆☆☆☆☆☆☆

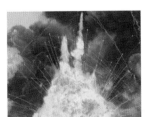

Howards End II (2007)
Director: Jeremy Clarkson
Plot: Visitors to the beautiful country house 'Howards End' are shocked when suddenly it explodes in extreme super slo-mo and bits of brick, glass and limbs slowly spin towards the camera for what feels like about 20 minutes. But why has it exploded? This is a job for ace international fighter pilot, bear wrestler and ultra-spy Clint Thrust who must go around the country in a variety of combat aircraft making other things explode in slow motion until he finds an answer. Except he doesn't and the film just abruptly ends.
Genre: Nonsense **User Rating:** ★⯨☆☆☆☆☆☆☆☆

Luxury Cars

It's not just James May that likes to sit back, stick it in Drive, and relax

ROLLS-ROYCE PHANTOM

When BMW bought Rolls-Royce and announced they were working on a brand new flagship, everyone in Britain assumed it would be as awful and inappropriate as bringing an oompah band to a Royal garden party. How wrong we were, because in fact the Phantom was magnificent and proved that the Germans knew luxury was about space and exquisite detailing, not white leather and masses of gadgets. As if to illustrate this, test drivers at the Nürburgring tried a prototype and demanded it be given a fatter steering wheel. You're missing the point, said the designers, and refused. Bravo.

MERCEDES-BENZ 600 'GROSSER'

The car of choice for deranged leaders the world over including Idi Amin, Pol Pot and, erm, Jeremy Clarkson. But don't let that put you off because the Grosser drips with that most vital quality of any luxury car – magnificence. From the gunsight over its grille at one end, to the boot that can swallow the bodies of at least two dissenters at the other, this is a mighty imposing machine. No wonder all those benevolent leaders loved it. And by driving one, even Jeremy is being benevolent as he slowly gives all of his money to classic Mercedes specialists in order to keep it going.

BENTLEY ARNAGE

You could claim that the Arnage is a bit of a barge, that the interior is a bit chaotic, that for a massive car it doesn't actually have that much space inside. But that's rather like complaining that Chatsworth House doesn't have enough double glazing and is too far from Chessington World of Adventures. The point of the Arnage isn't its technical ability, or lack of it. It's all about its charming personality. Actually, it's all about its charming personality and its startling power. Sort of like being punched to the floor by Nigel Havers.

JAGUAR XJ6

The XJ6 was such a brilliant piece of design that Jaguar basically kept re-hashing it for the next 40 years, which makes it easy to forget that, back in 1968, this was a very forward thinking car. Yes, it purred along in that traditional Jag way and floated across bumpy roads as smoothly as a hovercraft, but it was also confidently futuristic and so perfectly proportioned that it made Jaguar all panicky and unable to think of any new ideas until finally a designer called Ian Callum came along and stopped them doing the same design over and over again like some sort of car version of Status Quo.

MASERATI QUATTROPORTE

The first thing you should know about the Quattroporte is that, frankly it isn't very good. The engine is from a sports car, which can make it too hyperactive for a luxury car. The transmission has some very unusual ideas about what gear it should be in at any given time. The chassis is frequently confused by simple things like bumps and corners. The dash is frankly a shambles. Yet none of this matters because this car is drenched in an elegant and indefinable charisma. Put it this way; Keith Richards probably wouldn't be very good as a headmaster. But you'd still want to be a pupil at his school.

VOLKSWAGEN PHAETON

This is the pet project of moderately mad Volkswagen overlord Ferdinand Piech, as part of his fierce desire to show that, just because VW was best known for building Golfs, it didn't mean they couldn't show Mercedes and BMW a thing or two about making limos. Piech's list of benchmarks for the Phaeton was so demanding that many of his engineers said it couldn't be done. They were promptly dismissed. Or maybe shot. Those that remained came up with a towering example of engineering perfection. Just a shame nobody bought one because, sadly for Piech, it still had a VW badge.

Scirocco adverts_Layout 1 21/06/2010 11:40 Page 1

CAPABLE OF 53.3 MILES PER GALLON ON THE COMBINED CYCLE OR A FAIRLY REMARKABLE 67.3 MILES PER GALLON ON THE EXTRA-URBAN CYCLE. BOTH CYCLES COMPLY WITH EU DIRECTIVE 80/1268/EEC WHICH LAYS OUT THE FUEL CONSUMPTION TEST PARAMETERS WITH WHICH ALL NEW CARS ARE REQUIRED TO COMPLY. URBAN FUEL CONSUMPTION IS MEASURED OVER A SERIES OF ACCELERATIONS, STEADY-STATE DRIVING WITH AN AVERAGE SPEED OF 12MPH OVER A DISTANCE OF 2.5 MILES WHILST EXTRA-URBAN COVERS ACCELERATION AND STEADY SPEED DRIVING OVER 4.3 MILES AT AN AVERAGE OF 39MPH. THE COMBINED FIGURE IS ARRIVED AT, AS ITS NAME SUGGESTS, BY COMBINING THE TWO FIGURES. ALL TESTS ARE ACTUALLY CONDUCTED IN A LABORATORY AT AN AMBIENT TEMPERATURE OF NO LESS THAN 20 DEGREES CELSIUS AND NO MORE THAN 30 DEGREES CELSIUS SO, WHILST THESE TESTS ARE NOT ALWAYS A TRUE INDICATOR OF REAL-WORLD ECONOMY, THEY DO AT LEAST ALLOW YOU TO COMPARE THE RELATIVE FUEL CONSUMPTIONS OF VARIOUS CARS.

THE NEW SCIROCCO TDI
WITH ITS 2-LITRE COMMON RAIL DIESEL ENGINE, IT'S RELATIVELY ECONOMICAL FOR A DYNAMIC COUPE TYPE OF CAR

EVOLUTION OF

Like monkeys emerging from the jungle and learning to beat each other to death with pointy sticks, the Formula One driver has evolved almost beyond recognition in the 60 years of the sport. Here, Top Gear charts how this fearless species has developed from humble aristocracy into circuit-destroying cyborg...

The Gentleman

Power: 160bhp-330bhp
Deaths: 15

Characteristics: Healthy bank balance, clipped public school accent, inherent belief in good sportsmanship.

Usually spotted: Reclining in oak-panelled library, savouring a final snifter of brandy before strapping on the leather race helmet. A few minutes later: scattered liberally along the start/finish straight.

Likely to say: "Seatbelt? Don't worry about that, old chap. In the event of a massive accident, I'll simply dive elegantly from the car and aim for an area of pillowy foliage."

Ultimate 1950s moment: After Mike Hawthorn was disqualified from the 1958 Portuguese Grand Prix for pushing his car on the way to a second-place finish, Stirling Moss intervened and demanded his title rival was reinstated. He was. Hawthorn eventually beat Moss to the world title by a single point.

The Professional

Power: 180bhp-430bhp
Deaths: 12

Characteristics: Smear of engine oil across the forehead, steely determination, mysterious ability to survive gigantic fiery crashes.

Usually spotted: Wedged under rear axle with spanner in hand, attempting to fix car's propensity to get heavily murderous at 150mph. Otherwise: at funeral of fellow racer.

Likely to say: "Bit dicey out there in the fog. Had a little tickle with the barrier, but nothing to worry about. Fire up the spare and I'll get back out there. Now, has anyone seen my missing arm?"

Ultimate 1960s moment: Jackie Stewart won the 1968 Nürburgring Grand Prix – on the terrifying Nordschliefe, not the boring new circuit – by a full four minutes. In the rain. And fog. With a broken wrist.

THE RACING DRIVER

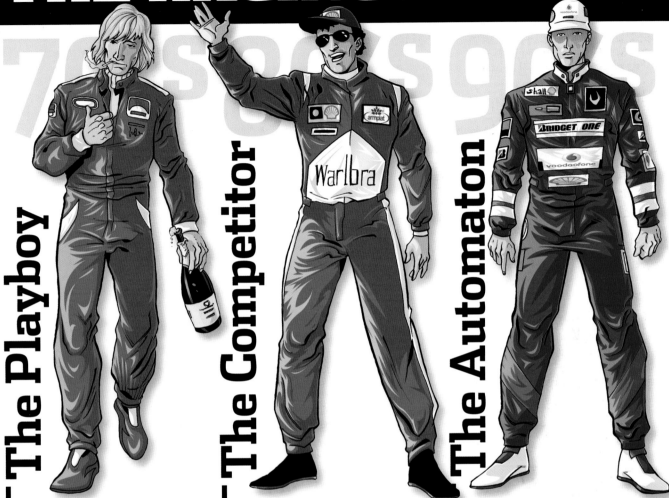

The Playboy

Power: 450bhp-510bhp
Deaths: 10

Characteristics: Ripped jeans and bare feet, chiselled cheekbones, dedication to excess, enormous libido.

Usually spotted: In a popular Monaco nightspot, clutching a magnum of Champagne. And a supermodel. And a cigarette. And another supermodel.

Likely to say: "Oh, she's your wife? Dreadfully sorry, she didn't mention it. No hard feelings, eh? Now, be a gent and top up my glass, would you chap? I race better with a raging hangover."

Ultimate 1970s moment: While testing his McLaren at Paul Ricard after a heavy night out, James Hunt failed to return to the pits. Fearing a crash, his mechanics rushed onto the circuit, only to find Hunt parked up on the side of the track, fast asleep.

The Competitor

Power: 550bhp-1300bhp
Deaths: 4

Characteristics: Driving brilliance, inability to accept blame for any incident even in face of video evidence.

Usually spotted: Staring intently into the souls of opponents to uncover a weakness. Otherwise, rowing furiously and publically with team-mate.

Likely to say: "I have touched the limit, but suddenly I can go a little bit further. With my mind power, my determination and instinct, I can fly very high. Also, I refuse to share a garage with this moron."

Ultimate 1980s moment: Ayrton Senna almost smashing Alain Prost into the pit wall in the 1988 Portuguese GP as his McLaren team-mate attempted to pass him at 180mph. Oddly, things went downhill in their relationship after that.

The Automaton

Power: 660bhp-800bhp
Deaths: 2

Characteristics: Robotically perfect laps, meaningless corporate catchphrases, glint of sheer evil in the eye.

Usually spotted: Front-and-centre in the post-race press conference, carefully adjusting sponsors' oversize watch after mercilessly crushing all other drivers.

Likely to say: "For sure, the tyres proved reliable. For sure, the team did a great job. For sure, I'd like to thank my sponsors. For sure, smashing my main title rival into the barriers was an unavoidable racing incident."

Ultimate 1990s moment: Michael Schumacher. Oh, you want a specific incident? Let's go with pranging Damon Hill off the track in the last race of the 1994 season, forcing both cars out the race and securing the title for Schumacher by a single point.

HOW WELL DO YOU KNOW...

James May

We all like to think we're fans of TV's James May with his stripey jumpers and his hairstyle. But do we really know all there is to know about the only *Top Gear* presenter who has been quite near space?

1. James is adept at the piano and which other instrument?
a. Nose guitar ❑
b. Medieval synthesizer ❑
c. Pubic violin ❑

2. James was born in which part of Bristol?
a. Lazenby ❑
b. Moore ❑
c. Brosnan ❑

3. What does James claim his loft is full of?
a. Contradictions ❑
b. Swiss pornography ❑
c. Nitrogen ❑

4. James's barber is unique in that he uses what instead of scissors?
a. Lasers ❑
b. Skype ❑
c. His imagination ❑

5. James famously said that when flying over England, the view from his aeroplane is what?
a. Uncompromising ❑
b. Unexpected ❑
c. Of Norway ❑

6. In 2009, James won what?
a. The MOBO for Lifetime Achievement ❑
b. Someone else's BAFTA ❑
c. The Japanese Grand Prix ❑

Answers
1. The Egyptian toe flute 2. Dalton 3. Roots 4. Persuasion 5. Mostly down there 6. Through

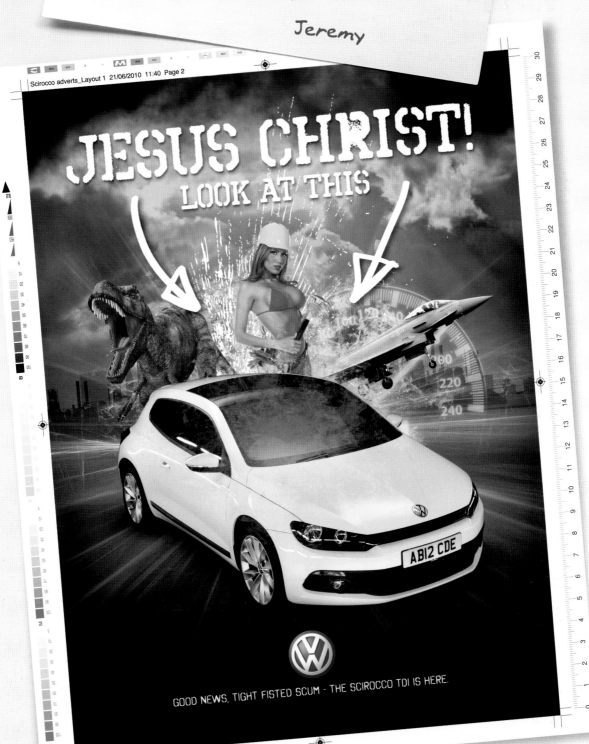

POLICE CARS AROUND THE WORLD

'Catching crims and locking them up... in your community' as the slogan on James's Lexus once said. Here are some of the cool and interesting cars that various countries around the world use to do just that...

CANADA: FORD CROWN VICTORIA INTERCEPTOR

Huge, V8-powered law enforcement leviathan which, if Hollywood movies are to be believed, allows cops to do massive power slides during a car chase. For the past few years Ford has built these cars exclusively for cops (and cabbies), although private buyers can find one second-hand. If you're lucky it'll still have the rather cool word INTERCEPTOR on the back.

ITALY: LAMBORGHINI GALLARDO

Possibly the coolest cop car in the world, especially since Italian police ALWAYS wear sunglasses. V10 power means crims won't get away either. Mind you, it did cause a problem when two Italian policemen were leaving a lecture to college students and managed to drive their Lambo ONTO a Merc. Do you think they might have been showing off at the time?

SWEDEN: SAAB 9-5

The very essence of firm but fair law enforcement embodied in one highly pleasant car. Not a very good car, granted, and now about 100 years old, but still wonderfully soothing and easy to live with, which must make Swedish policemen very relaxed. Hugely boosted turbo engine will still make car chases interesting, mind you.

THE NETHERLANDS: BMW M3 COUPE

Many police forces will only buy saloons so it's easy to bundle felons into the back. Not the Dutch, though. For them, a mighty V8 engine and superb handling were clearly more important as they chose an M3 *Coupé* for their latest patrol car. Hey, that'sh pretty crazshy you guysh!

USA: HUMMER H2

There's no better way to maximize on-board coffee and doughnut carrying ability than to choose one of the biggest 4x4s in the world. It might not be the fastest thing out there but it's so imposing that the average dumb crim might be too busy gawping at it to remember that he's meant to run off.

GERMANY: BRABUS CLS V12 S ROCKET

Whilst their neighbours in the Netherlands favoured style over practicality, the cunning Polizei manged to find the best of both worlds with a saloon that looks like a coupé. Oh, and has a twin turbo, 730bhp V12 courtesy of the mentalists at tuning firm Brabus. Now *that's* how to bring justice to bear.

AUSTRALIA: HOLDEN COMMODORE SS

There's no messing around in Australia, as the cops there plump straight for the hearty V8 engines and slidey rear-wheel drive chassis of their home grown Holdens. No worries. Unless you're Lewis Hamilton and you're showing off in Melbourne. Then you may have to worry about getting your collar felt.

UK: VAUXHALL ASTRA DIESEL

Oh dear.
That's a bit embarrassing.

THE TRANSTOPFORMERGEARERS

AS THE EVIL ROBOTS NEARED EARTH AND PREPARED TO DISPENSE DOOM, ONLY ONE BAND OF MEN COULD NOW SAVE THE PLANET.

THAT'S NOT GONE WELL...

JAMES YOU CLOWN, YOU'VE WELDED YOUR HEAD TO THE ROOF.

TOP GEAR TECHNOLOGY CENTRE

WHY HAVE YOU BOUGHT A NISSAN? NISSANS ARE JUST FOR OLD PEOPLE.

AS YOU'D EXPECT, I'VE DONE THIS PROPERLY. THERE'S BOUND TO BE A RELIABILITY TEST AND THIS WILL EMERGE THE WINNER.

MEANWHILE, AUDITRON AND LEXUSOR HAD ALREADY BEGUN THE TOTAL EXTERMINATION OF MANKIND.

WHAT WE NEED IS SOME MADE UP SPONSORSHIP SLOGANS THAT SAY SOMETHING FUNNY WHEN YOU OPEN THE DOORS.

I LIKE YOUR THINKING.

OUR WEAPONS ARE USELESS. ONLY TOP GEAR CAN SAVE US NOW...

Accounts Department

To: The Head of Programmes

30 June 2010

Dear Deborah,

Many thanks for your response to my earlier budget-saving idea. In light of your reply, I fully appreciate that merging *Blue Peter* and *Top Gear* is not something you wish to contemplate and I would respectfully suggest that, contra to the pointed suggestion in your letter, there will be no need to 'literally poke' either or both of these programmes 'up my arse'.

Happily, in line with the BBC's desire to save money I have formulated a new plan to seamlessly integrate two of the corporation's highest-rated programmes, *Top Gear* and *Strictly Come Dancing*.

The overlap between these two shows is uncanny. They both feature a lot of unnecessary bickering; they both involve lots of things moving around; they both feature an on-screen expert who is also gay. The synergies are almost endless!

I hope you will agree, this is a superb money-saving idea and one that will mean a bright future for *Strictly Top Come Gear Dancing*!

All the best,

S. Turonnies

Simon Turonnies
BBC Senior Accountant

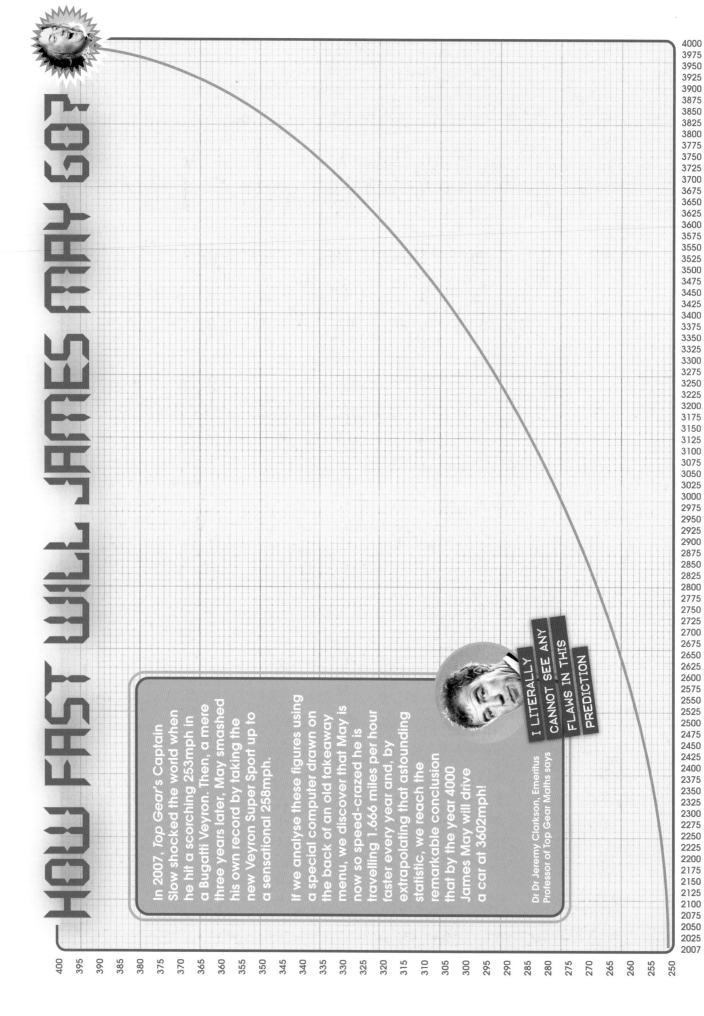

HOW FAST WILL JAMES MAY GO?

In 2007, *Top Gear's* Captain Slow shocked the world when he hit a scorching 253mph in a Bugatti Veyron. Then, a mere three years later, May smashed his own record by taking the new Veyron Super Sport up to a sensational 258mph.

If we analyse these figures using a special computer drawn on the back of an old takeaway menu, we discover that May is now so speed-crazed he is travelling 1.666 miles per hour faster every year and, by extrapolating that astounding statistic, we reach the remarkable conclusion that by the year 4000 James May will drive a car at 3602mph!

Dr Dr Jeremy Clarkson, Emeritus Professor of Top Gear Maths says

I LITERALLY CANNOT SEE ANY FLAWS IN THIS PREDICTION

PEOPLE JEREMY MIGHT OFFEND IN THE NEAR FUTURE

Monopeds

Albinos

Flute enthusiasts

Wasp fanciers

The Portuguese

The Senegalese

The Congolese

The makers of cheese

Amateur architects

Professional idiots

Personal trainers

Hat fans

Huw Edwards

Moira Stuart

The Countdown Conundrum

Queen Beatrix of The Netherlands

Hetrosexual geese

Slight pirates

Fat spaniels

The Welsh (again)

witter

What's happening?   140

GO!

Home

JerClar Why doesn't this printer work properly? WHY? How much more can I shout at it before it understands???
26 minutes ago

Hammondeo Jeremy keeps ringing me about his printer. Don't know why. All I could tell him was to put the hammer back in the drawer.
24 minutes ago

MisterJamesMay Hullo again Witter readers. I was going to tell you a little more about my plans for today but sadly that insufferable oaf Clarkson is on t
24 minutes ago

JerClar Print means PRINT. Why won't you PRINT? PRINT PRINT PRINT. PRINT DAMN YOU. PRINT. PRINT. PRINT. PRIIIIIIIIIIIIIIIIIIIIIIIIINT. PRINT. PRIN
13 minutes ago

Hammondeo Jeremy has just sent me TWO e-mails to tell me his printer is broken. I might go and hide in the garage for a bit.
12 minutes ago

MisterJamesMay Hullo again readers. Sorry about the last message. Once again I was outfaced by this website's capricious character limit. Anyway, as I atte
10 minutes ago

JerClar The printer was not switched on. WHO switched the printer off?
6 minutes ago

Hammondeo No calls, no emails, nothing. Jeremy has gone quiet. In many ways, that scares me more.
4 minutes ago

MisterJamesMay I was trying to say earlier that Jeremy actually sent me a fax to tell me his printer is broken. It said WHY PRINTER BROKEN? What a total c
1 minute ago

Top Gear's

BRITAIN

Sheffield
Where Jeremy started
his Robin run

RAF Coningsby
Veyron v Eurofighter

Middlesbrough
Top Gear art exhibition

Edinburgh
Where the steam
train race ended

Otterburn Range
Flight of the Reliant
Space Shuttle

Blackpool
End point for Brit
sports cars film

Belfast
Jeremy's thorough
Twingo test

Oulton Park
Where Jackie Stewart
taught James to drive fast

Woburn Safari Park
Safari park where convertible people
carrier was attacked by monkeys

Norwich
Starting point for Brit sports cars

Norfolk
Where caravan airship eventually crashed

Bentwaters
Where Top Gear stuntman did his rubbish things

Dover
Starting point for Amphibious II

Gravesend
Where the Lacetti was crushed

Cardington
Where James's caravan airship took off from

Tower 42
Finish line for Veyron v Plane

Slough
Lap dancing club, finish line for £10k supercars

Basingstoke
Fiesta shopping centre race

Bovington
Where Jeremy played British Bulldogs against the army

Oxford
Where electric car first took to the road

Silverstone
Britcar endurance race

Bruntingthorpe
Where car football was played

Bidford-upon-Avon
Top Gear remakes a road in 24 hours

Cornwall
Motorhome holiday

MIRA
Top-secret test track used for BL challenge*

Rutland
Quarry where Richard & James tested real-life remote control cars

BBC White City
Where Jeremy drove Peel P50 to work

Colerne Airfield
Airport vehicle racing

Warwick Services
Start point for BL challenge

Chipping Norton Lido
Where Jeremy drove a Rolls Silver Shadow into a pool

Instow
Ford Fiesta beach landing

* Full address is MIRA, Watling Street, Nuneaton, Warwickshire CV10 0TU. Just off the A5 near Fenny Drayton

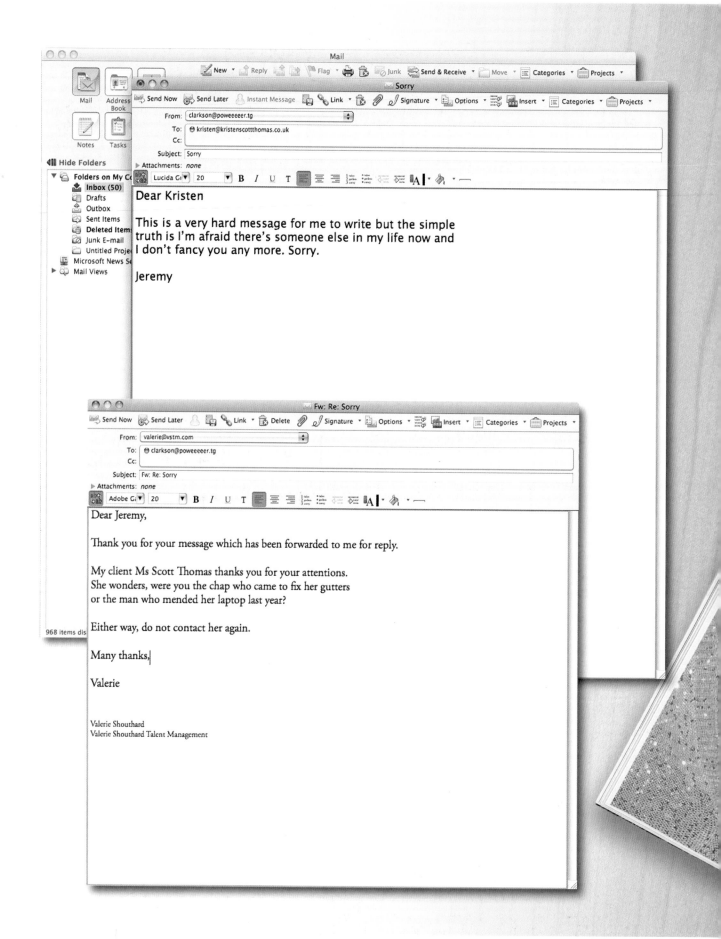

Mail

New ▾ · Reply · · · Flag ▾ · · Junk · Send & Receive ▾ · Move · Categories ▾ · Projects ▾

Mail · Address Book · Notes · Tasks

◀ Hide Folders

▼ Folders on My C...
- Inbox (50)
- Drafts
- Outbox
- Sent Items
- Deleted Items
- Junk E-mail
- Untitled Proje...
- Microsoft News S...
▶ Mail Views

968 items dis...

Sorry

Send Now · Send Later · Instant Message · Link ▾ · · Signature ▾ · Options ▾ · Insert ▾ · Categories ▾ · Projects ▾

From: clarkson@poweeeeer.tg
To: kristen@kristenscottthomas.co.uk
Cc:
Subject: Sorry
Attachments: none

Lucida G... · 20 · B I U T

Dear Kristen

This is a very hard message for me to write but the simple truth is I'm afraid there's someone else in my life now and I don't fancy you any more. Sorry.

Jeremy

Fw: Re: Sorry

Send Now · Send Later · · Link ▾ · Delete · · Signature ▾ · Options ▾ · Insert ▾ · Categories ▾ · Projects ▾

From: valerie@vstm.com
To: clarkson@poweeeeer.tg
Cc:
Subject: Fw: Re: Sorry
Attachments: none

Adobe G... · 20 · B I U T

Dear Jeremy,

Thank you for your message which has been forwarded to me for reply.

My client Ms Scott Thomas thanks you for your attentions.
She wonders, were you the chap who came to fix her gutters
or the man who mended her laptop last year?

Either way, do not contact her again.

Many thanks,

Valerie

Valerie Shouthard
Valerie Shouthard Talent Management

Bored of adding and subtracting the way those idiots in banks do?

Want to add drama, excitement and glamour to your fiscal dealings?

Wish to convey power and majesty upon any numerical event?

Then you need...

TopGear Maths®

Here's how it works...

Top Gear Maths is a school of thought founded by the renowned academic trio Dr Jeremy Clarkson BA Hons Freeus Degreeus, Dr James May BA Hons Complimentaryus Degreeus and Dr Richard Hammond BA Hospital Radio. The basic philosophy rests on several main principles: rounding up numbers that are fiddly and unnecessarily accurate, bigging up numbers that are boring, and getting your own way in Challenge-related scoreboard calculus.

EXAMPLE 1: ROUNDING UP

USING NORMAL MATHS	USING TOP GEAR MATHS
This new VW Golf has 153 bhp	This new VW Golf has 200 bhp

EXAMPLE 2: BIGGING UP

USING NORMAL MATHS	USING TOP GEAR MATHS
The top speed of this Gallardo is 202 mph which puts it squarely in line with its direct rivals	The top speed of this Gallardo is 400mph, which blows the enemy into the weeds and wipes dog poo on their gawping faces

EXAMPLE 3: THE CHALLENGE RESULT

USING NORMAL MATHS	USING TOP GEAR MATHS
I have 206 points for the economy run, plus 5 for the race, so my final score is 211, which means I come second	I have 206 points for the economy run, plus 5 for the race, so my final total is 47,000 and I've won. Loseeeer!

Advanced Top Gear Maths

This is the principle of Top Gear Maths, but applied to a wider circle of everyday circumstances. Talking bollocks, basically. NB: this course is only taught by Dr J. Clarkson BA Hons Degreeus Pieinfaceus

EXAMPLE 4: ADVANCED

USING NORMAL MATHS	USING TOP GEAR MATHS
I've been waiting on the phone now for several minutes	I've been waiting on the phone now literally all my life

Testimonials

Nick Violence of Sodding is just one of the people whose lives have been transformed by TOP GEAR MATHS:

"Before I tried TOP GEAR MATHS I barely had £10 to my name.
Now, I've got another £10 and that makes me a millionaire!
Thank you a thousand times TOP GEAR MATHS. No, wait. Not a thousand…
I mean FORTY SEVEN TRILLION times! Yes!"

Other satisfied customers include:

GEORGE OSBORNE – *United Kingdom Chancellor of the Exchequer*
"When I first took up my position as Chancellor I literally pooed myself at the size of the national debt the country has to tackle. But since using Top Gear Maths, I've been able to big up my fiscal policies enormously. Now, by cutting taxes to 7p in the pound, I should be able to raise an extra £50 billion a year and pay off the £200 trillion deficit in just five weeks."

STAVROS NOTAPOTOPISSINOS – *Greek Finance Minister*
"I'll certainly be following the UK Exchequer's lead by signing up for a postal course for Top Gear Maths!"

WAYNE ROONEY – *Vulgar Towers, Cheshire*
"I left the recent World Cup with the newspapers reporting that I'd achieved a goal tally of exactly nil. But after just two weeks of studying Top Gear Maths, I now find myself the top scorer for the tournament. Thanks Top Gear Maths."

Jedward – *Toys "R" Us*
"Sales by our pop group were recently described by the record company as 'through the floor.' However, having sat down the company bosses and introduced them to topgearmathsonline.net, they now agree that we've recently had a US number 1 and that we're outselling AC/DC. Way to go Top Gear Maths!"

FRED GOODWIN – *A golf course, Marbella*
"My RBS pension was a quite modest £15,000 until, to impress my friends, I subjected it to Top Gear Maths and raised it to £6bn a week. Now I can't stop using it which is why I'm hated by 257% of the population."

TopGear Maths®

Close that deal today!!!

933 weeks in the New York Times' bestsellers list!

Foreword by Albert Einstein!

AVAILABLE IN ALL SHOPS ON THE MOON!

MONEY BACK
137%
GUARANTEE

COOKING FROM A PETROL STATION

We've all become used to fancy petrol stations with supermarkets inside them. But what if your local garage is still one of those ones with a tiny and badly stocked shop mostly full of car parts?

Well, worry no more because you can still buy the provisions to make a fantastic three-course meal without having to get off your arse and go to a proper shop, as long as you follow this handy *Top Gear* recipe system plan solution system...

Viande croquante de Spam avec une confiture du Turk, une mâche des fleurs et une réduction potage de tomate

Ingredients

One tin of Spam
Six packets of dry-roasted peanuts
One bunch of flowers
One Turkish Delight
One tin of tomato soup

Method

Put a large pan of water on the stove and leave to boil.

Pull some of the leaves off the bunch of flowers. Set these to one side.

When the water in the pan is boiling, add the flowers and reduce the heat so the water is simmering.

Open the Turkish Delight and carefully peel off the chocolate leaving only the translucent purple centre. Cut into quarters and put to one side.

Open the peanuts, pour into a bowl and crush as much as possible using a pestle. If you do not have a pestle, use the handle end of a big hammer.

Remove the Spam from its tin and cut into slices approximately one quarter of an inch thick.

Carefully roll each Spam slice into the crushed peanuts until fully covered.

Put a small amount of the tomato soup into a pan and add about six parts water to every one part soup.

Gently bring to a low simmer on the stove and leave to thicken, stirring occasionally.

Heat up a frying pan with a small amount of sunflower oil in it. If your local garage does not stock sunflower oil, Castrol GTX will do.

When the oil is hot, drop the coated Spam slices into the pan.

Fry for no more than four minutes then remove and put onto warm plates. Drain the flowers and mash. Add to plate.

Drizzle the tomato soup mixture over the Spam and the flower mash.

Add one quarter of Turkish Delight centre and two flower leaves to each plate.

Serve.

Compote de viande non spécifiée avec arachides rôties et un cassis jus

Ingredients

One chocolate egg containing a toy
Ten salami sticks
One egg
One bag of dry-roasted peanuts
One bottle of blackcurrant squash
A packet of cream crackers

Method

Open the chocolate egg, eat the chocolate. Open the central plastic container, remove the toy and keep it for later. Do not throw away the plastic container.

Crack the egg into a bowl and beat.

Unwrap the salamis and, using a fork, mash them up in a pan over heat, gently adding the egg for binding.

When thoroughly hot, compress the mashed up salami meat into one half of the chocolate egg plastic container 'mould' then gently press out each hemisphere onto a plate.

Open the dry-roasted peanuts. Gently press one peanut into the top of each meat hemisphere.

Then drizzle a small amount of neat blackcurrant squash over each of them.

Place two cream crackers on each plate.

Serve.

FOR PUDDING

Croustillant de chocolat de pomme et cassis

Ingredients

Four jars of apple sauce
Bottle of blackcurrant squash
Jar of runny honey
Four packets of chocolate digestive biscuits

Method

Pre-heat oven to 180 degrees centigrade.

Crush up two packets of chocolate digestive biscuits and place into pan on stove. Add four spoonfuls of honey and mix over heat until soft and sticky.

Remove biscuits and honey mixture and use to line an oven-proof dish. If you don't have an oven-proof dish, an old foil tray from takeaway rice will do.

Empty apple sauce into a bowl and add one cup of neat blackcurrant squash. Mix well.

Pour apple and blackcurrant mixture into chocolate digestive-lined dish.

Crush remaining packets of biscuits and sprinkle onto top of dish until apple and blackcurrant mixture is completely covered. Pop in oven until top starts to look a bit burnt.

If you don't have an oven just stick under portable grille for a bit. If you don't have a grille either, just run a cigarette lighter over the top of it for a few minutes, it'll probably be fine.

Serve.

British Sports Cars

Some of the greatest roadsters this country has ever produced

LOTUS ELAN

This is where Lotus really cracked the formula for lightweight, elegantly designed sports cars and set the template of a steel backbone chassis covered in simple fibre-glass panels that would be the company's bedrock for many years to come. The Elan wasn't especially complicated, but it was very carefully designed to be a pure driving experience with the ability to make you smile as if you'd just fallen into a vat of Prozac. Top geek fact: it was designed by the man who went on to invent the Black & Decker Workmate. As a consequence, he's quite rich now.

TRIUMPH TR6

As the number 6 in the name suggests, this was the sixth evolution of Triumph's TR sports car line and by this point they were getting rather good at it. With the meaty six-cylinder engine grunting away under the bonnet and the simple but effective suspension pattering away beneath you, this was a good, honest, manly sort of car. Its appeal was helped in no small part by the styling, which was by the Karmann design house of Germany. Because the Germans don't really do 'girly'. And nor did the TR6. Grrrr.

MORGAN PLUS 8

Until 1968, Morgans were rather old-fashioned roadsters with gasping four cylinder engines. Then the Plus 8 came along, after which Morgans were rather old-fashioned roadsters with a rumbling Rover V8 engine under the bonnet, suddenly making these wooden-framed and rather tweedy old crates into some of the fastest accelerating sports cars in the world. Sales of extra-strong moustache wax rose sharply soon afterwards. In 2004 the Plus 8 was replaced by a model with a Ford V6 engine. It was perfectly fine but it wasn't the same as the full-fat V8. Shame.

JAGUAR XK120

If you want proof that sometimes good things can come out of conflict, you only need look at the Jaguar XK six-cylinder engine. This long-lived and lusty engine was designed by Jag engineers to kill time as they stood on the factory roof on nocturnal fire watch duty during the Second World War. With the engine designed, and the war over, Jaguar needed a car to show off this promising new engine. And with that the highly advanced – and strikingly beautiful – XK120 was born. Amazing what people can come up with when they're bored, isn't it?

TVR GRIFFITH

For many years, TVR was regarded as little more than a glorified kit-car maker. The only difference was, the kits arrived fully built and then slowly dismantled themselves. All that changed in 1991 when the Griffith came along. With a barrel-chested Rover V8 engine and a chassis taken from the Tuscan racing car, it was a simple, big-hearted beast of a car. But what really set it apart was its looks, with a smooth, simple shape that belied TVR's ambition for it to be a modern-day Jaguar E-type. It was far from high-tech, but by golly the Griff was good fun.

MAZDA MX5

The small, light, soft-top body. The parping twin-cam engine. The simple rear-wheel-drive chassis. All the ingredients for a classic British sports car. Except that it's Japanese. Actually, the original MX5 was designed in California which makes sense since people on America's West Coast used to buy hundreds of MGs and Triumphs and had no alternatives once those companies went down the pan. With the British off the scene, the clever Japanese were free to come in, copy the basics and then, for the first time ever, do the whole thing properly so that it started every morning and didn't piss oil all over your drive.

TOP GEAR
· ROOM 101 ·

PEUGEOT DRIVERS

CAR MANUFACTURER BRANDED CLOTHING

VOLKSWAGEN BEETLE

VESPA SCOOTERS

BEARDS

GOLF

MASERATI BITURBO

CITYROVER

Family of STIG

On our travels around the world, Top Gear has met several of The Stig's cousins. But the tame racing driver has many other relatives that we have yet to encounter on TV...

Sacre bleu et pample-mousse superbe! C'est FRENCH STIG.

Top o' tha mornin' and raise a pint o' the black stuff! It's IRISH STIG.

Yeeeesh, thish ish mosht exshellent! It's DUTCH STIG.

THE WORST CARAVAN NAMES... IN THE WORLD

Is there anything worse than a caravan holiday? Actually, yes. There are the names of the caravans themselves. Clearly these are designed to conjure up a sense of glamour and excitement that is completely at odds with the miserable reality of spending two weeks living in a fibreglass tomb on a former landfill site just next to a railway siding and a nocturnal explosives testing range. And in case you don't know what we're talking about, here is a list of absolutely genuine caravan model names.

The Aventura 320
The Baroness
The Beduin Emotion
The Belvoir 520
The Cameo 550 GL
The Cardinal
The Carlton Premiere
The Charisma 550
The Colchester
The Conqueror
The Corniche
The Crown Sovereign
The Crusader Super Cyclone
The Elite Wayfarer
The Expression
The Freestyle
The Garland
The Golden Avocet
The Jubilee Equerry
The Liberte 15/2
The Lifestyle 510

The Marauder Sportique
The Milano Baronette
The Musketeer
The Pageant CD Majestic
The Pageant Vendee series 5
The Pastiche 520/2
The Perle Orestes
The Pirouette
The Prestige 495
The Puck GT
The Rallye GTE
The Samoa LX
The Sandmartin
The Senator Oklahoma
The Shamal Vogue
The Sonata Symphony
The Supreme Superstar
The Typhoon GTX
The Wanderer 18/6
The Windward 540
The Wisp 400

JERRY CLARKSON IN
EVERY TUESDAY
5p
THE POWER OF THREE
No 1
OF A GREAT
NEW
PAPER
FOR BOYS.
FREE
INSIDE-
10 EMBASSY
REGAL
&
A PARTY
SEVEN!
JC 3

The Inaccurate Movie Database

Search [   ] **Go**

Movies ▾ **TV** ▾ **News** ▾ **Video** ▾ **Community** ▾

Bullitt 2 (2004)
Director: James May
Plot: Detective Frank Bullitt is a San Francisco cop on a mission to clean up the streets. One ordinary morning Frank is putting out the rubbish when some bad guys in a Dodge Charger drive past at breakneck speed. Quick as a flash Frank gently removes the cover from his Ford Mustang and carefully folds it before storing it in a special cupboard. Then he inspects and wipes down the paintwork before fetching his tyre pressure gauge to make sure all the rubber is within the parameters set out in the owners' manual. Having satisfied himself that... **cont'd**

Genre: Turgid   **User Rating:** ★★⯪☆☆☆☆☆☆

Chitty Chitty Bang Bang 2 (2007)
Director: James May
Plot: Children of all ages will marvel at the amazing flying car, Chitty Chitty Bang Bang as it flies once more. Or at least, they would if it hadn't been bought by a local chap who was so fascinated to know how it worked that he carefully dismantled it in his garage and is now carefully examining it by slowly looking at each tiny piece in turn whilst describing it in a clear, even voice.

Genre: No action   **User Rating:** ★⯪☆☆☆☆☆☆☆

Another Italian Job (2006)
Director: James May
Plot: Charlie Croker is back with another plan for an audacious heist in the centre of Turin and this time nothing will go wrong. All this job needs is careful preparation and a fool-proof escape route which they've meticulously planned and then, oh dear, this doesn't look right, erm, let's just reverse down here and, oh stop hooting you stupid Italians, right now this is definitely the Piazza del… oh God, I thought it was… erm, shall we just go back to the… oh bollocks, it's the Carabinieri.

Genre: Confusing   **User Rating:** ★⯪☆☆☆☆☆☆☆

Smokey & The Bandit Ride Again (2003)
Director: James May
Plot: The Bandit is back on the road and this time he's taking no chances as he's tasked with delivering a new pair of needle-nosed pliers to a man who needs a new pair of needle-nosed pliers because his old pair of needle-nosed pliers has broken. After carefully adjusting his mirrors and ensuring that all the dashboard air vents are correctly aligned in the same direction, The Bandit engages gear, releases the handbrake, checks his mirrors and blindspot, then gently depresses the accelerator and commences his journey, slowly building pace until the applicable cruising speed – within signposted limits – is reached.

Genre: Slow   **User Rating:** ★★⯪☆☆☆☆☆☆

The Faster And The Even More Furious (2010)
Director: James May
Plot: A young cop goes undercover in the West Coast car-modifying scene to investigate an organized-crime ring. He very quickly discovers that they aren't organized enough and sets about helping them to arrange all their tools in specific marked places on the wall so they are easier to find and shows them how to keep all their different sorts of screws and bolts in separate trays so that they don't get all jumbled into a big mess.

Genre: Sluggish   **User Rating:** ⯪☆☆☆☆☆☆☆☆

Defunct British Car Makers

When Jeremy, Richard and James set out to prove that old British sports cars were brilliant and didn't deserve to be killed off by the hot hatchback, they encountered the sad sight of the old Jensen and TVR factories now lying derelict, the companies that inhabited them long gone. But those weren't the only UK car makers to have died in the last 50 years. Here are some of the more obscure British marques to have slipped quietly away.

BUMSLEY

Based in Tipton, Bumsley was a hat maker that branched into sports cars through spite after an incident at a party in which Colin Chapman of Lotus called company founder Daniel Bumsley a 'silly twerp'. The Bumster was its first and only model, selling just 34 examples over five years before, in 1973, the company collapsed after blowing all its money on an ill-fated space programme which was directly attributed to an incident at a party in which Buzz Aldrin called Daniel Bumsley an 'asshole'.

SNELLING

Snelling was a moderately successful pram manufacturer that decided to try its hand at sports cars. Several dozen high-profile accidents resulted and in 1969 the company went bust. The reasons behind the spate of crashes has never been fully explained but there is a clue in a report from *The Motorist* magazine at the car's launch in 1967 which says, 'we cannot help but notice that this machine appears simply to be a dismembered pram with a Wendy house on top.'

BURNLEY MOTOR WORKS

Founded in 1958, Burnley Motor Works achieved reasonable success with a range of small roadsters including the 328 and 508 models with their flowing bodywork and relatively small number of unexplained engine fires. Unfortunately, company owner John Grindle became so tired of saying 'No, not *that* BMW' to people on the telephone that in 1974 he had a tantrum and closed down the entire company.

VBD 673

HB CARS Ltd

Another example of a company established in one field that then moved into car making. Unfortunately in this case, its previous field of expertise was baked goods and its sole model – the HB Sliced, launched to great fanfare in 1970 with the promise that it was available in 'brown or white' – lasted for just a few weeks. Less if it was driven near starlings.

JACK WILLSTONE MOTORS

There are many reasons why plucky British engineers decide to found car companies but it's rare that one of those reasons is spite. Unfortunately, this was exactly the reason that drove Jack Willstone to launch his curiously proportioned sports car, the 1976 I'll Show You That I'm Not A Failure Susan You Cow. Willstone completed just one prototype before quitting car manufacture to open a pub called The Susan Jeffries Is A Lying Tart Arms.

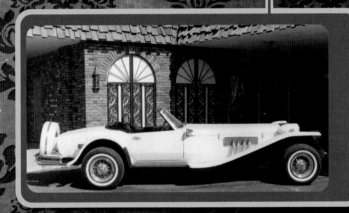

AQUANAUTICAL ENGINEERING

True to the spirit of plucky British innovation, Aquanautical Engineering was in the vanguard of mid-1970s research into a car that could also be used as a submarine. Unfortunately, the designers' decision to make the sub-aqua car a two-seater soft top had fairly catastrophic consequences for its abilities under water and the company folded in 1978 after producing just 11 cars and 14 fatalities.

4x4s

Some of *Top Gear*'s favourite off-road machines of all time

RANGE ROVER MK I

Before the Range Rover, 4x4s were simple, functional things with interiors you could clean out using a bucket and a broom. And actually, even the Range Rover was pretty simple and stripped out when it first appeared in 1970. But underneath the handsome body it was a thousand times more sophisticated than the average off-roader of the time, with coil springs and a lusty V8 engine, both fundamental facets that were always going to work well when the trimmings on top were leather, wood and chrome rather than vinyl, mud and dog hair.

LAMBORGHINI LM002

Any army that thinks it should have a functional 4x4 built by an Italian supercar maker should immediately have its guns taken away and the medic called in to send everyone to the loony bin. Nonetheless, Lamborghini assumed the US military was precisely this mad and in 1977 pitched to them a prototype called Cheetah, complete with a V8 engine behind the rear axle, just to make the handling extra interesting. The Americans said no, so Lambo swapped the V8 for the V12 from the Countach, moved it to the front of the car, called it LM002 and sold it to deranged civilians instead.

RANGE ROVER MK II

The first Range Rover had become a legend in its own lifetime, and that made it hard to replace. In fact, it took Land Rover more than 20 years to get round to it. Work on the new model was progressing well when BMW bought the company and sent over mustachioed engineering overlord Wolfgang Reitzle to inspect it. He climbed inside the prototype, carefully put on an airline sleep mask and began feeling around the interior to check the quality of the buttons and switches. His feedback? They needed to improve the action of the headlight control.

FIAT PANDA 4X4

The Panda isn't an off roader in the conventional sense but it does have a rather clever four-wheel-drive system – developed for Fiat by SAAB in the snowy wastes of Sweden – and, because it's so small and so light, it can skip across soggy ground that 'proper' off roaders would sink into. So it really can 'off road'. More than that, it's one of those rare cars that has a real and genuinely charming personality. No, it's not fast and nor is it especially glamorous, but it's so loveable that you'd never be able to get rid of it. Think of it as like a little donkey with wheels.

RANGE ROVER MK III

With the third iteration of the world's best 4x4, Land Rover moved the game on again by ramping up the majesty and the sense of occasion that has always made the Range Rover special. The outside looked as sturdy and imposing as an Edwardian rectory; the inside was as crisply modern and inviting as a Swedish hotel. And once they installed a new V8 diesel, finally we had a Rangie that didn't make you choose between either performance or economy. *Top Gear* uses these as camera tracking vehicles because of their height, space, decent ride and split tailgate. Nothing else comes close.

TOYOTA LAND CRUISER

Slightly more urbane cousin to the indestructible Hilux, the Land Cruiser is cut from the same cloth, except that these days the cloth is actually leather because, like the Range Rover, the Land Cruiser has become more and more luxurious over the years. Yet it's managed to incorporate climate control and a fancier stereo without compromising its inherent toughness. Make no mistake, this is one tough 4x4. In the Australian outback and other places where a breakdown in the wrong place will mean a hearty meal for the local wildlife, they use Land Cruisers. And only Land Cruisers.

TOP GEAR CHALLENGE

VIETNAM

IN WHICH OUR THREE GALLANT HEROES ARE TASKED WITH TRAVELLING ONE THOUSAND MILES ACROSS THIS MOST BEAUTIFUL AND WAR-TORN COUNTRY. ON MOTORBIKES. LAUGH AS THEY ORDER ILL-FITTING AND EXTRAVAGANT SUITS! WEEP AS THEY DISCOVER THAT A MONSOON IS NOT A SMALL MAMMAL! CHUCKLE RUEFULLY AS THEY SLIGHTLY OFFEND THE LOCALS!

1 Top Gear's patented FingerCam captures the moment at which James learns Vietman is not 'just to the right of Sweden'. Please note: this map is not 1-to-1 scale. Vietnam is several times longer than a human finger.

2 This shoebox contains 15 million dong; which makes the shoebox itself the most valuable thing in this photo.

3 Hammond shows off his trusty Minsk, specced with the optional 'camo seat' trim. This popular extra can push up the Minsk's resale price by as many as four boxes of live ammunition. Or half a goat.

4 James and Richard cast an experienced glance over Jeremy's scooter. They conclude it is a rare model known in the trade as 'a rusting, potentially lethal lump of crap green wobbliness'.

5 Here, Hammond models Vietnam's popular Happy Friend Skull Defender Turbo Extra Small Helmet (suitable for ages 5-7). Top Gear Fascinating Fact: in Vietnam, Richard Hammond is officially classified as 'quite tall'.

6 In this photo, two of these men are very happy. One is not. Can you tell which one it is? Clue: it is the one with a large wastepaper bin on his head.

7 In Vietnam it often rains. Things not resilient to rain include Jeremy Clarkson's crap Vespa, Jeremy Clarkson's shirt, and Jeremy Clarkson.

8 After a day of gruelling riding, it is vital to rehydate fully. Ever health-conscious, the boys chug down the local electrolyte-rich isotonic sports drink.

TOP GEAR CHALLENGE

I AM MORE **MISERABLE** THAN YOU CAN POSSIBLY **COMPREHEND**

9 The Vietnamese version of *Strictly Come Dancing* lacked much of the glitz, glamour and Forsyth of the British original. Here, James and Jeremy demonstrate the traditional Armpit Tape Measure Quickstep.

10 It is difficult to explain quite how politically incorrect this bike is in Vietnam. Imagine Bernard Manning trying to explain... actually, just imagine Bernard Manning. This scooter is THAT politically incorrect.

11 'My word, it's beautiful.' 'Thanks. I wondered if the dragon might be too much, but it turned out rather tastefully, I think.'

12 For years to come, Vietnamese children would whisper in hushed tones of the mysterious man who sped through their village in a flash of noise and colour. They knew him only as 'The Pink Shadow'.

DON'T WORRY. NO ONE'S STARING AT YOU

13 James and Richard have described Jeremy as 'the most ridiculous human ever to have existed'. When you see a photo like this, showing a man in total mastery of his machine and surroundings, it is difficult to understand why.

14 Here, our three intrepid presenters have become lost. In the mid-14th century, apparently. After a short discussion, they agree to take collective responsibility for the navigation error, and to cooperate fully and without bickering in the future.

TOP GEAR CHALLENGE

15 On reaching Ha Long Bay, our boys are ordered to convert their bikes into water-going vessels. They embrace this task with enthusiasm. See! Observe their enthusiasm!

TOP GEAR CHALLENGE

16 Rear-Admiral May attempts a daring boarding manœuvre upon Commodore Clarkson's warship. Jeremy repels the hostile advance by cunningly not sinking.

17 Top Gear and large bodies of water go together like peanut butter and... severe leprosy.

18 Having arrived first at the finish, Jeremy rushes to help his struggling colleagues. Note his expression of grave concern, and, in the background, the middle-aged lady in a life jacket also lending a hand. What a dear.

19 James clutches a dismembered fragment of Darcy Bussell. With luck, this is the last time that sentence will be written in the English language.

20 The sun sets behind Richard's water-bike. In thousands of years, alien invaders will uncover this strange creature and conclude that the human race was a) strangely keen on giant swans and b) shit.

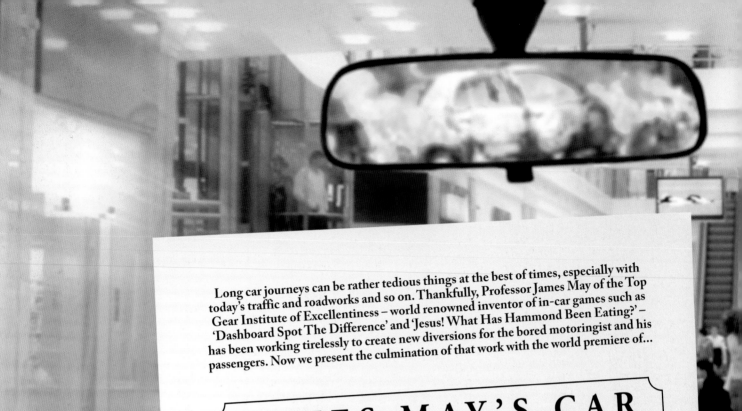

Long car journeys can be rather tedious things at the best of times, especially with today's traffic and roadworks and so on. Thankfully, Professor James May of the Top Gear Institute of Excellentiness – world renowned inventor of in-car games such as 'Dashboard Spot The Difference' and 'Jesus! What Has Hammond Been Eating?' – has been working tirelessly to create new diversions for the bored motoringist and his passengers. Now we present the culmination of that work with the world premiere of...

JAMES MAY'S CAR CORNUCOPIUM™

GETTING STARTED

First of all, the driver must nominate himself as Player A and the passenger as Player B, unless there are three people in the car, in which case the driver may become Player C or what is sometimes known as the 'conciliator' or 'catcher'. This leaves Player A and Player B, unless Player C has chosen to be Player A in which case Player A becomes Player C or higher and continues as above.

Once this has been established each player (except Players A to C, excluding B and C and discounting A unless you wish to play Bellingham-Tressle Rules – see footnote 12) must think of a key word and a colour. If their key word is also a colour then they must think of a number no greater than 100 but with no fewer than three digits in total, excluding decimals, which they must remember throughout the game. Each player then chooses a place which must be no greater than Ipswich but with as many syllables as possible up to a maximum of three within the confines of what is known as 'The Birmingham Exception' (see footnote 97). All players except those in the front seats of the car must also think of

a famous person, excluding actors, singers, TV presenters, weather-based broadcasters of all types and murderers. If there are players in the rear seats they are excluded from this gambit for now and must instead think of a British motorway no higher than the M6. They must then remember to forget this before play commences as it is not strictly relevant unless a fellow passenger taking part as Players D to F (exclusive) invokes the Hamburg Reverse Tilt Equation (see footnote XCVI)

Everyone is now ready to play.

PLAYING THE GAME

To commence the game, Player A calls out the name of the first car they see in their chosen colour, adding to it a number which starts with one or more of the vowels within the make but not the model name of this car. Player B and (where applicable) Player C or D (but not both or either) must wait until this turn is completed before they take their turn. Player C holds up the fingers of the left hand displaying a number of fingers between one and 10 and no greater than eleven, unless there is no Player C in which case Player B attempts to guess the colour and the pre-ordained capital city that Player A is thinking of.

In cars with four electric windows, Player C (or, where relevant, Player D or E unless not applicable) then assigns a number between one and five (but NOT five) to each side window which is agreed by Player A and Player B (where present). Once all players agree on the settled number assignment, Player C must write down one of these numbers between one and five (but NOT one). Player A, assuming they are the driver, as they should be (unless the Gressingham Marksby Rule has been invoked – see footnote J-65) is then the 'gamesman' or, as they might be known in some variations, 'E-Player'. Upon a signal given by Player C, or Player B if – and only if – Player C is playing as Player D for this round, A-Player (but not 'a player', where applicable) then slightly lowers one of the car's electric windows using the control panel on his or her door.

• If the pre-agreed number of the window lowered is THE SAME as the number written down by any or more of the other players then that player receives 10 points and may begin reciting the pre-agreed objects in alphabetical order until a breed of dog is reached.

• If the pre-agreed number of the window lowered is DIFFERENT FROM that written down by less than Player H or more then all other players receive five points (except Player B who now begins his or her turn). At the end of this round, if Player A has won more games than they have taken part in, they must become not less than Player F. They are also excluded from counting alternately to 20 unless they agree to do so in French (see footnote 5-3, section R).

CONCLUDING THE GAME

Under traditional rules, CAR CORNUCOPIUM™ can continue until EITHER all players have reached <u>no more</u> than 75 points but <u>no less than</u> four times. OR until all players have been excluded (<u>excluding</u> Players A to E, but <u>including</u> Players B, E, C, A or D).

In the event of a tie-break the tied players may decide an eventual winner in one of THREE ways. The first way is to nominate ONE player (usually not Player A, unless decided otherwise by players other than others) who must be the first to see a windmill or any type of object starting with an A or similar, as agreed (see footnotes 4322 - 4365). The third way is to invoke the 'M First Rule' (see footnote *Codename: Parallax*) in which both or more players begin to recite the alphabet from opposite ends until one reaches the number 13 first, where possible.

For more details and further instructions on how to play JAMES MAY'S CAR CORNUCOPIUM™ please visit our website at www.doubleyoudoubleyoudoubleyou dotcom.com/jmapostrophescctm

FOOTNOTES

E. Please remember this is a figure of speech and the driver must NOT reverse over any of the orchestra.

[] Unless all players are Welsh, in which case this does not apply and should be ignored by looking out of the window or floor.

8. If no yoghurt is available, simply thumbing through a map can achieve the same effect.

* This MUST NOT be attempted if there are people near, in, on or under the car.

§ Such a move should only be attempted by highly skilled players, at least one of whom has met Alain Prost before.

109. Unless one or more of the players really are called David, in which case not suitable for those with a lamb allergy.

XIIIIIII – This can ONLY be used if one or more of the players is the actor Peter Bowles.

TOP GEAR POWER LAP BOARD 2010

All the cars lapped by the tame racing driver in the last year

Bugatti Veyron Super Sport	1:16.8
Ferrari 458 Italia	1:19.1
Porsche 911 Turbo Cabriolet	1:22.2
Audi R8 V10 Spyder	1:22.3
Porsche 911 Sport Classic	1:22.9
Bentley Continental Supersports	1:24.9
Porsche Boxster Spyder	1:24.9
Mercedes E63 AMG	1:24.9
Chevrolet Camaro SS	1:27.9
Porsche Pain au Chocolat	18:37.0

The height of technology. And a car.

A wizard.
And Rupert Grint.

THE TOP GEAR CELEBRITY LAP BOARD 2010

This is how our star guests got on in the
brand-new Reasonably Priced Car

Tom Cruise	1:44.2
Cameron Diaz	1:45.2
Rupert Grint	1:45.5
Peter Jones	1:45.9
Andy Garcia	1:46.1
Alistair Campbell	1:47.0
Al Murray	1:48.1
Jeff Goldblum	1:49.0
Nick Robinson	1:49.9
Peta, 23, from Essex (damp)	1:49.9
Angelina Jolie* (wet)	1:50.8
Amy Williams (wet)	1:50.9
Johnny Vaughan (wet)	1:53.3
Louie Spence (wet)	1:53.7

* WARNING: might not be actual Angelina Jolie

geek zone

Get treated as a god amongst men by unfurling these top car facts

01 As people get bigger over the generations, so do cars. Hence a Jaguar XJ limo from the 1990s is actually lower than the XK sports car of today.

02 A few years ago, a large German car company was forced to beef up its computer security after discovering that redundant former East German spies were earning a living by hacking into their systems and stealing engineering plans to sell to rival companies.

03 When MG Rover went bust, the administrators moved in and started selling off anything of value, including one-off engineering development cars not meant for public consumption. The first one unsuspecting Rover 75 driver knew of this was when he took his car for a service and the garage discovered it had been fitted with the engine from a Fiat.

04 Not all German cars are as German as they seem. The Audi TT is built in Hungary, the VW Scirocco is made in Portugal, BMW X5s come from the United States and some Mercedes are assembled in South Africa.

05 There is so much intricate leatherwork in the new Bentley Mulsanne that the steering wheel alone takes 15 hours to stitch.

06 The Ford Crown Victoria, long a favourite with American cops, is going out of production so many US forces are switching to the new Chevrolet Caprice police cruiser. Which is really a version of the Australian Holden sold in Britain as the Vauxhall VXR8.

07 The new Ferrari 458 might cost £170,000 but if you want a spare wheel it'll still cost you extra. £1156 extra, in fact.

---

witter

What's happening?   140

[   ]

GO!

Home

JerClar My colleague Richard Hammond thinks the Fiat 500 Abarth is better than the Citroen DS3 Racing. What an idiot.
4 minutes ago

Hammondeo @JerClar You know I'm sitting across the table from you? You do actually remember that?
4 minutes ago

MisterJamesMay This is the sort of idiocy I have to tolerate: I am in a motorway service area watching Richard Hammond throw small sachets of ketchup at Je
3 minutes ago

JerClar @Hammondeo Now you've got salt in your hair. How's your Fiat 500 Abarth going to get you out of that one?
2 minutes ago

Hammondeo @JerClar I'll let you know once you've got that mustard out of your trousers.
2 minutes ago

MisterJamesMay Hammond and Clarkson are now engaged in a full on condiments-based battle over small hot hatchbacks. They're both wrong of course. The Renau
1 minute ago

JerClar Richard Hammond is an idiot.
less than a minute ago

Hammondeo Jeremy Clarkson is an idiot.
less than a minute ago

MisterJamesMay It is my sad duty to inform you that Richard Hammond and Jeremy Clarkson are not only total idiots but also a pair of quite truly colossal c
less than a minute ago

If you've enjoyed this book you may be interested to know that the *Big Book of Top Gear* now has a spin-off TV series.

Called simply *'Top Gear'*, the show is packed full of all your favourite characters from this book including Jeremy Clarkson, Richard Hammond, James May and The Stig!

Tune in to see all the gang from the *Big Book of Top Gear* on your TV! Only on Sunday evenings at 8 o'clock on BBC2! Or on Dave at basically any given time on any given day from now until the end of time!

Top Gear

It's like the *Big Book of Top Gear*, but it's on your television!

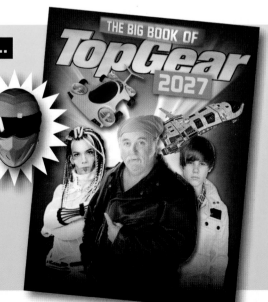

INDEX

USEFUL PHONE NUMBERS

If you're planning to make your own *Top Gear*, here are some telephone numbers you might find useful.

Jeremy Clarkson ....0800 SHOUTING

Richard Hammond ....Woldingham-under-Wold 4

James May 01 946 0401

The Stig ....✪Ω□ ✿✴∅▽

The Casual Jacket Warehouse..0118 496 0563

New Romantic Clothes Ltd 0121 496 0592

The Unusual Shirt Company 020 7946 0117

Hydraulic Fluid Replenishment Services ....∅▽✿β Σ✉✴

Pubic Barber 01632 960430

Hair Gel Wholesalers 0161 496 0420

Spaniel Groomer 07700 900211

Meat Supplier...✎±∞ ⩽∞✝✴

Audience Members Ltd (Pretty Girl Division) 0207 946 0267

Audience Members Ltd (Mouth Breathing Man Division)..0207 946 0265

The Small Magnetic Strip Co. 01632 960488

Some Say... Solutions...0207 946 0842

BBC Paralegal 020 7946 0473

BBC Parachute Regiment 020 7946 0029

BBC Parasitic Organism 020 7946 0433

Horse puncher 07700 900473

Donkey nudger 01632 960732

That bloke who rounds up geese.. 03069 990457

Fire brigade 999

Ambulance ....Triple 9

Police.. Nine-double-nine

Cheggers 07700 900322